COLLINS NUTSHELL BOOKS

Public Speaking

PHYLLIS BENTLEY

COLLINS
LONDON AND GLASGOW

GENERAL EDITOR: J. B. FOREMAN, M.A.

First published 1964

Contents

CHAPTER 1

General Approach

Perhaps I had better first declare my own qualifications for writing this book.

For thirty-eight years I have made public speeches, chiefly literary lectures, in considerable and growing numbers every year.

At first, as I have recorded in my autobiography, I lectured only locally, and in the oddest places: Sunday schools where choirs were practising above, or coal being cracked below; village halls on windy hill tops; among the planks and wheelbarrows of temporary premises; beside stifling oil stoves; beneath the light of one dim incandescent gas bracket. I lectured to Co-operative women and chapel members and school literary societies; then I broke into women's luncheon clubs and large evening groups; and presently was placed on the list of the then best known lecture agency in this country. Under these auspices I lectured in Scotland, in Ireland, in Wales, in England north and south. I also undertook two brief lecture tours in Holland, speaking in different towns to some six groups of the Nederlande-Engelande Association. Presently I made my first lecture tour in the United States; I failed there at first but later conquered, and made four more tours; travelling across the vast country east to west from New York to California and north to south from Seattle and Chicago to New Orleans. I have faced audiences of eighteen hundred and tiny groups of seven, and received every kind of welcome, from empty benches and whispering audiences to halls so crowded that people stood in the aisles and crouched on window sills.

I say all this merely to indicate that this book is not a theoretical dissertation, but a down-to-earth practical manual based on years of very varied—sometimes comic, sometimes wretched, sometimes highly enjoyable—experience of public speaking.

There are four essential qualifications for every public speaker.

The first is a thorough knowledge of, and affection for, the subject to be spoken about.

There is something of a fashion nowadays for " briefing" speakers, that is for some expert to inform an ignorant speaker of the facts he ought to know. I disapprove of this practice, which I regard as fundamentally insincere. I am told it is bound to operate in politics, but I do not agree. That statistics should be collected and put into suitable form for a minister by the civil servants of his department is proper, but the theme of the speech, the overall policy which he is advocating, should be thoroughly well known and believed in by the speaker.

It sometimes happens that a mayor, and still more often a mayoress, has to welcome guests or open institutions of which he or she knows little. In that case it is well to begin by admitting this, then proceed to the facts provided, and finally give your own personal view. If, for instance, you have to welcome a conference of electronic experts, you might say something on these lines: " Electronics are, I am sorry to say, a good deal of a mystery to me. But what a powerful mystery! There are, I am told (here give all the facts about electronics and the conference which have been marshalled for you). . . . So I feel, as we all must feel, that the future will be moulded by these forces which the genius of man has released. The deliberations of this gathering will therefore be of real importance to future human lives; I welcome the members most sincerely to our town and hope that they will have a thoroughly happy and successful conference."

Such a speech will be liked because it can be believed. Insincerity, pretence of any kind, are instantly visible in public speech, and audiences dislike them intensely. In fact, there is nothing they dislike more. Mistakes, hesitations, repetition, long-windedness, inaudibility are more readily forgiven, and arouse less hostility, than insincerity, and if you do not know your subject thoroughly you are bound to be insincere.

If, therefore, you mean to speak about pigs, or local government finance, or the poetry of Wordsworth, or abstract painting, you must know pigs, finance, Wordsworth, or abstract painting thoroughly well, and have some strong feeling about them; love them or hate them or want to improve them, it does not matter which, but be devoted to them. For what right has anybody to get up and harangue an audience, unless he has something he really wants to say?

This leads me to the next qualification: a devotion to your audiences and a desire to serve them.

A very popular writer and lecturer once said to me in a tone of fury: " Don't you despise your audiences? I do! " I exclaimed in horror: " You don't mean that! " He assured me that he did; but in fact he had just completed a long and enormously successful but frightfully exhausting lecture tour in the United States, and his nerves were in tatters. If he had really despised his audiences he could not have been a successful lecturer. For on the platform, as in ordinary life, you tend to receive what you give; give sincerity, friendliness, honesty, eagerness to explain, and you will receive friendly willingness to listen in return. Of course it would be tremendously exciting to tell your audience frankly that you hated them, but they would immediately hate you; unless you soothed them, police would soon have to be called in, and even if you soothed them, resentment would still lurk at the bottom of their hearts. Before going on to the platform, then, think to yourself: " These people in the auditorium, after a hard day's work, have washed and dressed and taken a bus, or driven and parked a car, and paid earned money, and are sitting in rows on rather uncomfortable seats, to hear me; I owe them my best." Unless you can thus put yourself into the frame of mind of charity for all men, I think you should keep off the platform.

The next qualification is a clear and carrying voice.

A powerful, resonant voice is not nowadays so essential as it used to be, since microphones are in very general use; but even today not every hall has a public-speaking system. The techniques for speaking without and with a microphone differ considerably and I will take them in turn.

First let me say that if your voice is weak, and your pronunciation blurred and uncertain, speech training from a qualified elocution teacher is advisable. But much can be done to improve your speech without recourse to paid assistance.

Let us take speaking without a microphone, first.

Stand up straight. Hold the head well up. Speak on the lower register of your voice, particularly if you are a woman. Look at the back of the hall, and speak to the back of the hall, to a point just above the heads of your audience. Try to speak from your lungs, *not* from the back of your throat. Open your mouth well. If you have any resonant quality in your voice, let it ring out, particularly in the first few sentences, but do not shout. Don't drop your voice at the end of your sentences. Vary your pace to avoid monotony. When you are well into your speech, adopt an easy conversational tone. For emphasis, speak more slowly and pause a little. But this must not be done too often.

If there is a microphone provided, the problem is different.

However much you dislike using a microphone on a public platform, if it is provided I advise you to use it, for the audience is accustomed to its use, and will not believe that they can hear you without it. I remember once declining to use a microphone in a tiny room with less than fifty luncheon club members present. I am used to making myself heard in large halls to several hundred people, and the acoustics in this little room were perfect, but I had hardly uttered a sentence before members began popping up to say they could not hear. I dislike the microphone because it cramps my style; I cannot walk about the platform, or drop my voice suddenly, or increase its volume or hurry my words. In fact, I can say more words in a given time with a microphone than without one; but with less emphasis and less effect.

If you are to use a microphone, see that it is set at the right height for you, not too high lest it block your face from view, not too low lest you have to stoop to it. The audience will be restless and impatient while this adjustment is being made, but never mind; better to keep them waiting and have the position of the microphone right than hurry the adjustment and be inaudible. A friendly smile to them while you are waiting may ease the situation. With a microphone, resonance is not required, indeed it is fatal; it makes the mike boom and crackle. A quiet, rather restrained tone is the thing, with a fairly even tempo of speech. Stand up straight, speak *at* the microphone but not closely *into* it; don't move your head or your body much from side to side, or your voice sound-waves will miss the microphone and be inaudible.

If you have any opportunity of practising these two

11

different modes of speech, take it eagerly. Neighbourhood halls may be open from time to time for repairs, or for preparations for some function, and the management may perhaps allow you to practise your voice for a few moments. Of course you will feel ridiculous both when asking for this favour and when bellowing away to a scattered group of amused workmen and waitresses, but don't let this deter you.

If you own or can borrow a tape recorder, speak a paragraph into the tape and play it back and listen to it. I warn you in advance that this is extremely disheartening. To begin with, on a tape recorder one's voice never sounds like one's voice; and all one's defects of speech are all too terribly audible. But if one knows them, one can at least struggle against them. I remember once hearing myself on a recorded broadcast. Among other defects I noticed that my pronunciation of the letter " s " was altogether too hissing and noticeable. I tried to conquer this, and I think I improved my " s " to some extent. A tape recorder reveals the " er "s and " um "s which we all use so frequently. Count them! You will be overcome by shame when you find how many you use in a paragraph; but shame is the first step towards reform.

Notice that I said " speak " a paragraph to the tape recorder, not " read " one. In the discovery of speech defects, reading will suffice; but speaking and reading are very different; speaking is, or should be, much more free and varied and changeful than reading, for speaking is the spontaneous expression of a thought which has just entered the mind. Reciting, i.e. uttering words learned by heart, has also quite a different effect from speaking. Reciting in a public speech is to be deplored except when a quotation is being made. The public speaker must be able to speak impromptu.

The fourth essential qualification is, therefore, fluency.

Some people are born fluent; words roll rapidly from their lips without apparent effort. I envy them; I do not really find it easy to express my thoughts quickly in suitable words. But fluency can be encouraged by practice. A good way to practise is this. Every evening, in the loneliness of your room, stand up, say firmly aloud: "Mr. Chairman, ladies and gentlemen," and go on to utter aloud a brief account of what you have done that day. Don't stop, don't pause; drive yourself onward. Make yourself finish your sentences; if you get involved in subordinate clauses, extricate yourself somehow. After a week of this you will have improved so much that you will continue the practice. After a month you will probably feel a good enough impromptu speaker to inflict your evening speech on a sympathetic member of the family.

At this stage it is a good idea to time yourself. The B.B.C. counts about 130-150 spoken words to a minute, but the natural tempo of speakers varies, and it is essential to know your own. Count five times 150 words in a book, read them aloud, note whether they take you five minutes, or more or less time, to say. Time your evening speech. Learn a piece by heart, recite it and time your recitation. Try, that is, to get the *feel* of how much time you are using. Speakers whose speeches are too short are felt not to give value for money; speakers whose speeches are too long are a fearful bore. However carefully you have prepared your speech, circumstances beyond your control may necessitate alteration. Chairmen may go on for nearly half an hour, or stand up merely to sit down; trains loom; tea cups begin to be heard in the neighbouring room and the audience's minds wander; on the platform the secretary may suddenly tell you a duration for the speech different from your expectation. You must *know* how you are getting along for time, without upsetting the audience's concentration by looking at your watch.

Perhaps I may be forgiven here if I mention one factor in successful public speaking, which I personally consider important. The audience, whether of fifty or five hundred or fifteen hundred people, are obliged to look at you for anything from twenty minutes to an hour. They are obliged to look at you because if they don't look at you they won't hear you well. It is your duty, therefore, in my opinion, to give them something agreeable to look at. Of course different modes of dress are agreeable to different types of audience. Some like the dressy, some the beatnik, some the neat and clean. I am not suggesting that you should conform to their wishes, or diminish your own individuality in any way; but do try to give them the best appearance of which your personality is capable.

Women should in all cases avoid downturned hats with large brims. However charming these may look from the front view, from the sides they act as screens; the face of the speaker becomes less visible and the voice less audible when thus screened. Since two thirds of the audience sit on the wings and only one third more or less directly in front, big brims are a major error. Also, may I advise against jangling bracelets? At first rather charming, the jangle soon palls. Nothing in the dress should be fidgeted with, as this makes the audience restless, so avoid long strings of beads, furs, stoles, etc., unless you can be sure of keeping your hands still.

Hands are indeed one of the worst problems of the public speaker. What are we to do with them? Let them hang loosely at our sides? This is a counsel of perfection. Some speakers clasp them behind the body (I do), some in front; some lean a few fingertips gracefully on the table. Men sometimes put one hand, or even both, in their pockets, and this has a rather friendly, homely effect.

Remember that all movement by a speaker distracts the audience's attention from words to movement, and try to avoid fidgeting if you can. Relevant gesture, movement with a purpose, is another matter; we shall discuss that in a later chapter.

CHAPTER 2

Think of Your Audience

Any housewife will tell you that the time to decide the size and shape of a jelly is while the jelly is still liquid. It can be poured, at that stage, into any mould and will take that shape with ease. But when once it has set, chopping pieces out to make it conform to the size of the serving dish ruins its symmetry, leaves unexplained yawning gaps in its pattern; altogether, when offered it looks a mess.

This homely metaphor applies very accurately to any well prepared public speech. The speakers who are really good impromptu speakers need not trouble to read this section; they are equal to any sudden demands and can lengthen or shorten the exposition of their argument at will. But very few people indeed are good impromptu speakers, and it is wise to assume, at any rate at first, that you are not one of them. The speakers who appear to speak impromptu, with light-hearted ease, are usually those who devote most time to preparation. Often after a lecture members of the audience have said to me wistfully: " How nice it must be to be able to speak so *easily*, without any *trouble*." I always tell them the truth, that in fact I take a great deal of trouble; they smile incredulously.

The first thing to do in preparing a speech is to discover, if possible, into what mould it should be poured, in order to give the greatest satisfaction and information to your audience. Some secretaries of organisations give this information spontaneously; from some it emerges in correspondence; from others it can only be found out in talk a few minutes before you go on the platform.

The lecture agencies which have arranged lectures for me added to their booking forms, in response to agonised cries from me and no doubt others, a question about duration (and also, I may say, about dress. I begged for this because once, turning up for an evening lecture in a velvet suit, I found everyone in dinner jackets and airy cocktail dresses. Floodlight poured upon my insignificant and ill-clad person, as I felt it to be, and confidence oozed from my toes. Nowadays this is not the problem it used to be, since dress is altogether simpler and less formal; but as I have said in the previous chapter, the lecturer should try not to disappoint his viewers' expectations in appearance).

The question of duration is extremely important. You can say something useful in any length of time from ten minutes to two hours, provided you know beforehand what duration is required. For a luncheon speech, thirty to forty minutes is a customary length; for an evening lecture, one hour; for an after-dinner speech anything from ten minutes to twenty, according to your position on the toast-list and your importance to the organisation. But the most astonishing variation of these customary limits can occur. I remember once making the inquiry from the chairman as we walked up the platform steps together at the meeting of an evening literary society: " About an hour, I suppose? " " Oh, we break for coffee after three quarters of an hour, and then have three quarters of an hour more lecture afterwards," she beamed. This, of course, is probably the worst possible way to arrange a lecture, for continuity is broken, you have to " get hold " of your audience twice and provide two climaxes, while during the interval members come up and ask privately questions which should form part of a public question period at the end. I had the length of time occupied by two stairs and the Chairman's introductory speech, to rearrange my material. Fortunately she spoke at some length. So never, never, begin a speech without knowing accurately what duration is required.

That is particularly important both for luncheon clubs, where members are due back at work, and for evening meetings, where last buses exercise an inexorable closure. If you have forgotten this matter until you are actually on your feet, it is better to make the inquiry then, rather than forge ahead in ignorance. " I'm so sorry, madam chairman, but I forgot to inquire what time this meeting wishes to close. Two o'clock? Thank you." If the meeting is a regular routine meeting, its members will not usually resent this, but on the contrary feel safe with you; at a grand celebration however they may feel insulted that you did not pay their great affair sufficient attention before.

A good way to enlarge a speech at short notice is to give more examples of the fact you are stating; if you are describing a country's climate, for instance, give two entertaining examples of its heat or cold instead of one. To contract a speech at short notice use the reverse process.

Another very useful item of knowledge—indeed it is almost indispensable to the inexperienced speaker—is the probable size of the audience. This is relevant to the amount of material necessary. Why? Because far more words can be said to a small audience than to a large audience. Why? For purely physical reasons. Small numbers of persons occupy less space than large numbers, and the speaker's words reach them more quickly. A faster pace can therefore be employed. To a small audience an easy, intimate, cosy manner is the best; one chats along comfortably, and may use dashes and brackets, so to speak, interpolations and digressions, without any ill effect. A large audience requires a rather more leisured and more formal mode of address. Speak too quickly to a large audience, and they do not hear you; speak too slowly to a small audience, and you appear stilted and dull.

The question of presence or absence of microphone is also important for the same reason. As I indicated in chapter one, more words to the minute can be spoken and heard if a microphone is used. In a large hall with no microphone the speed of delivery must be quite considerably slower than if a public-speaking system is present. Mercifully the chairman's introduction serves to reveal whether the system is in working order. But nowadays the microphone usually works; the days of booms and squeaks and sudden inexplicable switchings off are over.

It is very necessary indeed to know the *kind* of audience you are to address. Is yours to be a public lecture, open to all? Or is the audience some kind of group? A school? Undergraduates? Teenage? Adult? A learned society? A literary (or political or artistic or sociological) club? A group of business men or women? A male audience? A female audience? Mixed? Foreign?

Your tone and even your material should vary to suit the type of audience addressed. The pleasantest audience is of course one interested in your own greatest interest. For me, a literary society or an authors' club has this qualification. I can use technical terms to such audiences which would be quite out of place with others, and we share in common certain problems and certain ways of looking at life. A difficulty arises for me with other types of audience, unfamiliar or less familiar with literature, as it will for you in similar circumstances. Certain things must be explained to them, and yet you must not appear to be " talking down." Absolute sincerity, and a desire to serve your audience, will usually carry you through, but audiences detest being " talked down " to, and sometimes it is wise to say frankly some explanatory sentence. " May I just say what I mean by . . ., so that we shall not misunderstand each other." Or: " Forgive me if I am telling you something most of you know; I just want us to be quite clear about it before I go on to . . ." Phrases like: " as you probably know," " as I expect you know," and so on, are useful, for some of your audience are sure to know the fact in question and rejoice in their knowledge, others are just as sure not to know and are glad to have their ignorance enlightened without being exposed.

A " group " of any kind is easier to talk to than a public audience whose members are unknown to each other. In the presence of strangers, people—particularly English and Scottish people—are apt to be rather wary and reserved at first; this is an additional barrier which has to be broken down. You will rarely get a public audience with no particular unifying motive to laugh at the first paragraph of your speech, and to make a joke which falls flat is something of a disaster. So modify your speech accordingly.

As regards laughing: men laugh in public far more easily than women. Also men laugh more loudly than women. Men throw themselves about and roar with laughter if they feel like it, whereas women, more modest or timid or strictly educated perhaps, give only a genteel titter. I have tried the same funny story on both in the same town, and I know. (Younger people of both sexes burst into a sudden startling roar.) A laugh, by the way, always causes a slight disturbance; people sway slightly, causing a slight rustle, and some repeat the joke to others who have not heard it. As they say on the stage: time your laughs; that is, don't cut them. The most enjoyable audience to address, as regards sex, is a mixed one; the men start the laughter, the women follow; while a slight appreciative or horrified gasp from the women impresses the men.

Obviously the words and examples you use must be adapted to the age and intelligence of your audience. I am always rather apprehensive when I am asked to address a whole school, for the difference in power of comprehension between junior and senior forms is sharply marked. In public audiences the level, not so much of intelligence but of experience in your subject, may also vary considerably; you must observe very sensitively the response to your opening remarks and gauge the level required.

A learned society is of course an entirely different matter; the finest resources of your intellect must be employed, and your language should match. I remember once addressing a meeting of the P.E.N. (an international authors' society), in Holland I believe, about narrative in fiction. Because the audience was composed of various nationalities, I used simple words. A German said to me afterwards that my remarks were truly original and significant. But an English newspaper commented that I had spoken in too naïve a manner for such a conference. Here I was caught between two desires: to be understood by persons to whom English was not their native speech, and to match my words to the intellect of the audience. I had chosen the wrong one.

In fact, long words of Latin origin are more readily understood by most foreigners than simpler, more Anglo-Saxon terms, Latin being the common source of the French, Italian and Spanish languages. For example, " illumination " means more to most members of these nations than does " light." To foreigners, speak a little more slowly than usual, and with great precision, i.e. finish your sentences neatly. Long wandering sentences are very difficult to follow; so are digressions and parentheses, and joking idiomatic expressions. In general, continental Europeans and Americans both prefer a rather more formal and lofty style of address than do English people. Many Americans think indeed that they prefer a homely style, but I am doubtful of this; I remember a small-town

21

American teacher who after hearing a very learned Oxford professor lecture exclaimed in disappointment: " I understood every word he said! "

Certainly we must not distort our natural manner in order to give pleasure. But we all have differing modes of speech which we employ without thinking in differing situations; we speak differently to a parent, a spouse, a child, a lawyer, a friend. We are entitled to reflect upon, and choose, a mode of speech which will communicate what we have to say to our audience most clearly and agreeably.

If only secretaries and organisers would tell us what we need to know about our audiences! They do not seem to realise that they would get far better service from us if they did. Of course, they are not always able to tell us. I remember once visiting a university (redbrick) to give a lunchtime address. I had asked my correspondent to give me some hint as to the probable size of the audience, but received no information; on arrival I pressed the matter again. He replied that he had no idea. " When it's the Vice-Chancellor, of course, it's six hundred," he said, " but sometimes it's nearer sixty." Assessing my own drawing power at about seventy-five, I began hastily to remodel my notes in my mind during luncheon, only to find, when I was ushered at last through the tall curtains, some three hundred students assembled. Flattering but very confusing. The probable size of a political meeting is similarly not easy to gauge.

But if secretaries do not inform the speaker of the audience's requirements, that does not excuse the speaker from being reticent about his own.

Do you require a projector for illustrations? Do you require assistance in showing these? Do you require a screen, or will you bring your own? A map? A blackboard? Chalk? A piano? An accompanist? A table?

A darkened room? Even if you have visited the organisation on a previous occasion, do not assume that your wants will be remembered, for often the secretary is a different person.

You should also inform the secretary of the time of your arrival in the town, and of your means of transport; also the time of your departure and your means of transport, and any professional speaking engagement you may have on the following day. You will find your travel arrangements made much easier by this frankness.

CHAPTER 3

Preparing the Speech

Speakers of natural eloquence, who can make good speeches impromptu, without preparation, are fortunate; they are also few. Many speakers *think* they can do so, but they are mistaken. Nothing is more tedious and ineffective than a speaker who rambles on, or thunders on, without displaying any consecutive line of thought or logical argument. The Prime Minister William Ewart Gladstone, a noted orator of the Victorian era, often spent a day, we are told, lying on a settee and " wombling " a coming speech, and we have all heard anecdotes of the preparation Sir Winston Churchill devoted to his magnificent speeches. In fact, the more preparation you have given a speech the more easily you can deliver it, and the more spontaneous it will sound; practice will enable you to speak in an increasingly free and lively way. Men, by the way, are often much too careless in this matter; with cheerful self-confidence they make no preparation at all, feeling sure they will "get through somehow." Women, on the other hand, are apt to be too meticulous, learning their sentences by heart. Both results are lamentable; for the men, chaotic, for the women, stilted.

Any kind of speech or lecture must " follow a charted course," to quote Sir Winston. Not only must it have a definite beginning, middle and end, it must go somewhere; that is, it must say something, and each part must lead logically on to the next.

THEME

First of all, then, sit down and consider carefully the point you want to make. Why are you making this speech? Do you want to persuade your audience on some point? To persuade them to some action, or dissuade them from some action? To communicate some information? To express some point of view? To thank somebody? To open a bazaar, a school? What aspect of life are you trying to illuminate? The smallest speech, on the most general occasion, must have a point, an aim, a theme, or aimless and uncharted wanderings and fearful boredom will ensue. For remember, listening to speeches can be terribly boring. A friend of mine who often has to act as chairman to visiting lecturers tells me that she sometimes counts the "k's" in the lecturer's words—it is her only means of keeping awake! *You* have to combat this boredom; it is not the audience's job to stay awake, but yours to keep them awake. First, then, decide your theme. Let me give a few examples.

Why I belong to (believe in) this or that political Party.

Wordsworth's poetry is so superb that you would enjoy reading it.

This town needs a Repertory Theatre.

The Government's economic policy is sound (or unsound).

It would be good for us to form a cricket club.

We have no facilities here for a cricket club and should join that of the neighbouring town.

What modern schools should contribute to the modern world.

The meaning and purpose of Founder's Day.

We need a new church organ.

We do not need a new church organ, but should send the old one to be repaired.

I want to interest you in some discoveries recently made in bio-chemistry.

Let me just make the matter quite clear. The *subjects* of the lectures mentioned above are: a political Party; Wordsworth's poetry; provincial repertory theatres; present economic policy; cricket clubs; modern schools; Founder's Day; church organs; recent bio-chemistry. But the *point* of them, their *themes*, are given above, and all the material in the lecture should be arranged so as to lead up to this point, this conclusion. Thus no useful work can be done on the speech until this theme is settled.

THE BEGINNING OF THE SPEECH

Title of Speech

Say at once what your subject is. If the Chairman has already announced it correctly, begin: " As your chairman has told you, my subject tonight is . . ." Very often, unfortunately, the chairman either does not announce it, or he announces it incorrectly, or he speaks about it (confusingly) at some length. (I will deal with Chairman's speeches in the next chapter.) You should never, of course, be rude to a Chairman, but sometimes it is absolutely necessary to correct him. Do this as pleasantly and affably as you can. " I'm afraid my subject does not have quite such a wide scope as you kindly suggested, Mr. Chairman . . ." Sometimes you can slip in the correct title by saying: " In speaking to you tonight on The Swaledale Breed of Sheep . . ."

Speaker's Qualifications

Next, if the Chairman has not already done so, say briefly

why you have a special knowledge of the subject. This is a tricky business; you must not sound conceited, yet it is right that the audience should know your qualifications. If you have lived twenty years in Egypt, you have some right to speak of Egypt; if you have entered international skating competitions for ten years, you have some right to speak of skating; if you have been to the United States six times and travelled in forty-four out of the fifty states there, you have some right to speak of their varying landscapes and modes of life; fifty years on the stage, or six months on an iceberg, confer qualifications. If you are a really celebrated person and your chairman is a good chairman, he will have said everything necessary about you in his introductory speech, and if this has happened, do not say anything about yourself unless he has praised you more than you deserve. Then you must (again very affably) correct him. " I'm afraid it was only *two* gold medals, Mr. Chairman; I missed the third." But be sure to be brief on this point; audiences hate boasting, it arouses a feeling of hostility in them at once.

Special Appeal of Subject

Now comes a very important section. Say why the subject is worth talking about, and what especial appeal it has to the audience you are addressing, if any. Is the subject topical? Has it some local relevance? Has new material been discovered recently? Here are some examples for differing audiences.

1. " Thousands of Swaledale sheep are sent to market in Yorkshire each year, so the subject is of vital interest to all farmers in the North Riding." (*Farmers' Association.*)

2. " The wool of the Swaledale sheep, once used for woollen cloth, is now in great demand for carpets, and therefore I

feel the curl and consistency of fleeces are of special interest to all carpet manufacturers." (for *Carpet Manufacturers*.)

3. "In recent years a great deal of new material has been discovered about the Brontës, material both psychological and sociological." (for any *Yorkshire Group*.)

4. "Although the Brontë sisters lived quiet, private, un-eventful lives, and the century since their death is crammed with great writers and literary masterpieces, their fame to-day continually increases. Plays about them . . . novels . . . radio and television serials . . . library use . . . booksellers' sales." (for *Foreign Students*.)

5. "The Brontës have given us a series of daydream writings of immense psychological interest. These have as yet been insufficiently studied, and it is my hope that I may tonight interest you in and perhaps stimulate you to the necessary research." (for *Psychology Faculty*.)

6. "With a General Election only three weeks away . . ."
(for *Political Audience*.)

You will, I think, perceive the purpose of the variations in the Introductions 3 and 4, if you consider the audiences to whom they are addressed. The people of Yorkshire, in which Haworth is situated, know a great deal about the Brontës before you begin to speak, so you must convince them that you have something new to tell them. Foreign students need to be sure that the Brontës are still of importance in English literature, and therefore worth their study.

If you cannot think of any reason why your subject should be of special interest to your audience, you really ought to have chosen—or the organisation ought to have chosen—a different subject.

Opening Words

Let me warn you of two important points in the beginning of your speech. The first is this: do not utter anything of vital importance in your first words, for the very important reason that many of your listeners will not hear them. The chairman has just finished speaking and sat down. There is always a rustle, a ripple of movement, a settling of handbags, a re-crossing of knees, when the audience is released from the courtesy of listening. The larger the audience, the more formidable can this rustle and ripple be. There is one very famous example of this. One of the finest speeches in the world, that of Abraham Lincoln at the dedication of the cemetery at Gettysburg—the speech in which he uttered glorious words—" with malice towards none, with charity for all . . . a new birth of freedom . . . that government of the people, by the people, for the people, shall not perish from the earth . . ."—was disregarded and thought unimportant at the time, though it was later saluted everywhere. The truth is that Lincoln was probably not fully heard. A colleague, Edward Everett, had just completed a very long speech and seated himself. Lincoln arose and without any introduction uttered at once, in three brief paragraphs, this supremely beautiful speech, to which he had given hours and days of thought. Through the rustle and the ripple and the change of voice, he was not fully heard, and by the time he began to be heard, the speech was over. So: utter a couple of sentences before you bring out your key point. A short introduction, a short pause, and *then* you can say:

" I want to tell you at once that I . . ."

" Yesterday I stood on the docks at Malta . . ."

" The story of the Brontës begins with . . ."

Of course, rules of this sort are made to be broken if you have a personality or a story strong enough to override the consequences. If when you rise you can cry out something really startling:

" Yesterday I was at Cape Canaveral and saw the moon rocket launched . . ."

You may then secure an instant hush. But even so, some of your audience will not have heard you, and will anxiously consult their neighbours as to what you said; you will be obliged to say it again.

The other point on which I wish to warn you is the use of an opening anecdote. A relevant anecdote is a good opening, though even with this you must preface it by a few words. " Sir Winston Churchill remarked on one occasion . . ." or " A few years ago *Punch* published an entertaining article which told the story . . ." By a relevant anecdote I mean, of course, one which really relates to the subject of the lecture. You must be able to follow your anecdote by explaining why you told it, why it is helpful. " This was only a joke, of course, but it's a joke which serves to remind us . . ." or " I think you'll agree that this is exactly the attitude we should take about. . . ." Audiences like relevant anecdotes, which often make a point very clear. But audiences hate irrelevant anecdotes, anecdotes lacking connection with the subject, dragged in just to be funny. This is particularly true of women audiences, I think. I have seen them gazing with disgust at a speaker who opened by cheerily telling an irrelevant funny story.

Proposed Treatment

When you have announced your subject and explained your qualification to speak on it and its special interest, say how you mean to treat it.

" I want first to explain how this situation arose, and then discuss what methods we should adopt to deal with it."

" The questions I am about to ask myself and try to answer on your behalf, are these."

" I want to trace for you the life-story of the Brontës as modern research has given it to us."

The audience likes to be taken into your confidence in this way. It is relieved, too, to know that it is not going to be embarked on an aimless flood of oratory, but conducted along a planned course by knowledgeable hands. Those members who particularly want to hear what you have to say on a certain point, will not now wonder impatiently when, if ever, you are going to reach it; you have explained to them that it is coming under question four. The intelligent members will follow your scheme as you go along, and enjoy thinking: " Ah, here comes part three." They all feel that you know your subject and have taken trouble to prepare it; they respect competence of this kind and feel confidence in you. Reporters, too, find it easier to take down the speech when they know what to expect from it.

So the outline for the *Introduction* to your speech should look something like this; with the specific notes attached.

Introduction Title of Subject.

Why I have special knowledge of subject.

Why it is interesting to this audience.

(? Anecdote.)

Scheme of Lecture.

THE MIDDLE OF THE SPEECH

Headings

This is, of course, the heart of the matter. If you have an orderly mind, trained in logical presentation, you will probably be able to write down at once the main headings

—three or four for a short speech, seven or eight for an hour—of your material. But if you have little experience in this kind of work—and after all, there has to be a first time for everyone—you may find it best to jot down, in very brief notes, everything which comes into your mind about the subject, and then sort these jottings out into logical sequence. For a long speech, take a separate sheet of paper for each heading which comes into your mind, and enter each note on its appropriate sheet. During this process the headings will merge and divide and change so that you will have a real mental tussle over their arrangement; but, remembering that your conclusion must contain an emphatic statement of your theme, to which each heading must lead, you will eventually get your headings into order.

If your material can be arranged chronologically, or geographically, that is a great help. It will be easy for you to remember, and for the audience to follow.

Let us take some examples.

I have often lectured on the Brontë sisters. The points which chiefly interested me about the Brontës were: the interaction of their Celtic heredity with their Yorkshire environment, their childhood writings, their novels. Having "wombled" these matters a good deal, I finally wrote down as rough headings: Parentage, Haworth, Daydreams, Writings, Literary Career. I saw that these were chronological sections, and added headings to make the life-stories complete. Eventually the headings for this lecture ran:

1. Introduction. (If I was speaking to foreign students or audiences I stressed the continuing importance of the Brontës to English literature. To English audiences I stressed the new material. I told both I lived only ten miles from the Brontës' home.)

2. Celtic (1777-1820).

3. Yorkshire (1821-   ).

4. Daydreams (1826-   ).

5. Education (1831-1842).

6. Literary Career (1845-   ).

7. Sorrow (1848-1849).

8. Solitude and Society (1849-1853).

9. Marriage and Death (1854-1855).

10. Conclusion: Unique quality and worthwhileness of the Brontës' writings.

On the other hand, a lecture entitled *An English Woman in America* was best treated geographically; my headings were New England, Chicago, the Middle West, the Far West, Hollywood, the South, the Deep South, and so on, with general deductions about the American character and ethics for conclusion.

An abstract subject like *Character and the Novelist* can also be treated chronologically, i.e. you can begin with the observation of human beings, proceed to the creation of fictitious characters from them, discuss how names for these are found, and conclude by describing how you put characters into words. *The English Regional Novel* is a subject which can be treated either chronologically or geographically. I had a great struggle with myself over this, as I felt the temptation to slip from one arrangement to the other, which I knew would create muddle. Eventually I decided that literary groups would prefer the chronological method, for they would be interested in the development of the literary form, but foreign students and non-literary audiences would prefer the geographical arrangement, as what they wanted to know was what books to read to get an idea of the different parts of England. To this second lecture I gave the title *England in Her Fiction*, and though the material of the two lectures was the same, it was differently arranged and differently angled; the themes were different.

This rearrangement of material to suit the audience is part of the service a speaker should be eager to give.

Such subjects as *The Canals of England*, and *My Adventures in Russia* could also be treated either chronologically or geographically, according to your material and the point you are trying to make.

But unfortunately all subjects do not fall into easy arrangements of time and place, and then the problem of the selection and arrangement of your headings becomes difficult. Political speeches are particularly awkward in this respect, I think. The usual kind of election speech, the theme of which is: *Why you should Vote for This Party*, might be divided into four or five sections, each dealing with one particular point on which you agree with your party's policy—foreign policy, United Nations, domestic economics, education, taxes, for example—and perhaps one or two sections where you violently disagree with the opposing party. But these sections are all separate subjects; you must try to arrange them so that they tie up together and emerge as a coherent and consecutive policy.

Nobody but yourself can arrange the main contents of your speech for you, but some general hints may be useful, provided it is understood that there are few hints or rules which apply to all subjects; discretion and sense must be employed in adapting them to your own material.

It is important to rise to a climax. If there are several small subdivisions in your material, try to arrange it so that a couple of quick small subdivisions lead up to one big one. Don't have too many small divisions in your scheme; group them into two or three big ones. The biggest climax should come, of course, in your final section, but a slightly less emphatic climax should support and invigorate the middle of the speech.

When you have decided upon your headings, write them down in very brief form, not more than one or two words, and number them, so that they will be easy to learn by heart—e.g. I. Introduction, II. Celtic, III. Yorkshire, and so on. Headings arranged chronologically are easy to remember; for others not so arranged, invent some mnemonics (system designed to aid the memory) for yourself. The initial letters of the headings are often useful for this, especially if they chance to spell a word. " T'Sunwacdd " still recalls to me the names of the main rivers of Yorkshire, which all flow into the Ouse except the northernmost Tees, and " pelmssci " the reasons for the rise of the wool textile industry in the West Riding of Yorkshire. P for Pennines; E for east; L for limestone; M for millstone grit; S for sheep; S for streams; C and I for coal and iron.

Examples. Now consider your examples and illustrations. Nothing is less effective than a string of statements unsupported by examples, and examples always give colour and human feeling to a speech. If you are stating that Yorkshire has always been a sheep-growing county, give some examples. The West Riding of Yorkshire place-names Skipton (sheep-town) and Shipley (sheep-lea) occur in Domesday Book, 1089, and tell their tale. In 1292 the monks of a West Riding abbey, Kirkstall, made a contract to sell all their clip (sheep's fleeces) to the weavers of Milan for ten years. In 1303 Earl de Lacy, a noted West Riding landowner, had three thousand sheep in Yorkshire. How these examples, these illustrations, light up and make real and vivid the bald statement! Put these down very briefly under the appropriate heading:

Sheep 1089 D.B.: Skipton, Shipley.

1292 Kirkstall.

1303 Lacy 3000.

Whether you use one or three examples will depend on the duration required for the speech.

If you are giving a speech referring to Old Age Pensions, look up exactly when they were first given and how much, and all the subsequent dates and amounts. If you want to make the point that they are too small, give an example, well worked out, of a weekly O.A.P. budget. If you think that an increase is impossible for financial reasons, state exactly what such an increase would cost.

Anecdotes. This is the place, by the way, for the relevant human anecdote, amusing or sad as the case may be. Historical subjects do not lend themselves easily to such illustrative anecdotes, but sometimes one has a bit of luck that way. When walking along a Pennine lane one glorious spring day, I saw an old man repairing a dry stone wall, and called out: " Fine morning! " He gave me a look of contempt and replied: " Well, don't let's get into a lather about it." This admirable illustration of the Yorkshire dislike of excessive expression was just what I wanted for my Brontë lecture, to illustrate the clash between their Celtic heredity and their Yorkshire environment. But let me warn you against *inventing* suitable anecdotes. They always ring false, and are never as interesting as true stories. If you are entitled to lecture on a subject, that is if you are thoroughly acquainted with it, incidents will have happened to you in the course of that acquaintance, that study, which will serve as anecdotal illustrations. I will not say that illustrative examples and illustrative anecdotes will make the success or failure of your speech, but they will certainly affect its interest and its impact.

Quotations. If you are using any quotations in your speech, now is the time to check them carefully. It is morally wrong (because it is a lie) to misquote, so to ensure accuracy, quotations should either be read to the audience or be recited, i.e. learned by heart. Whether to read or recite quotations is a moot point. A friend of mine who gives more than three hundred lectures yearly in southern England, chiefly to Women's Institutes, tells me that her audiences like her to read quotations to them; they enjoy the feeling of being in touch with learned books. But I find that my audiences (chiefly urban) prefer not to be read to, unless the quotation is too long to be recited in comfort. So your experience and judgment must decide.

Quotations lend variety to a speech, for the rhythm and tempo of another person will naturally differ from your own. But do not use too many quotations. I remember that after I had lectured for the first time to the women's luncheon club in my native town and was feeling rather pleased with myself, the senior secretary—a friend and a very fine person of considerable worldly experience, whose opinion I respected—said to me: " I don't much care for quotatious lectures, you know." It was a horrid shock, but a salutary one. Of course in a literary lecture quotations are one's illustrative examples, and therefore must be used. But even in a literary lecture quotations can become a bore as a repetitious act, or disturb the main line of the argument if they are too frequent or too long. Too long a quotation is a bore anyway; the feeling of being held up, stuck on the record, irritates the audience.

Transitions. One of the great difficulties of speech-making is to pass gracefully, easily and logically from one division of the speech to the next. As I have said, I personally like to announce these transitions, as I think audiences enjoy knowing where they are. Therefore, I am not at all averse to using simple forms of transition such as the following:

" That was the end of my time in Zanzibar, for next morning suddenly . . ."

" We now come to the most important section of this difficult subject."

" That, I think, answers the third question. Now for the fourth."

" Those were the causes of the outbreak. Now let me describe its course."

If you feel that such " joinings " as these are unsophisticated, invent others for yourself. But be sure you invent them. If you prefer to go straight on, do so, but be sure you know the first sentence of your next section very accurately.

THE END OF THE SPEECH

The ending of the speech is of very great importance, for probably it is this which the audience will remember best. The concluding paragraphs should sum up, clinch, epitomise the whole talk. A fine quotation, if absolutely relevant, exactly on the spot, makes a good ending. If you mean to use your own words, you really must shape them thoroughly in your mind, and say them aloud to see how they sound. A feeble finish does irreparable harm to your speech and your reputation as a speaker. Have we not all seen speakers who after a pause and a gape, suddenly sit down? The audience is left let down, dangling. A certain feeling of anticipation, of drawing to the close, should be felt by both speakers and audience, and shown to some extent in the speaker's voice. But don't start this change of tone too early, or you will create either an irritation—" How long is he going on, playing on my feelings? "—if you maintain the tone, or an anticlimax if you cannot maintain it. " I thought he was going to finish minutes earlier." " He didn't know how to stop." " He should have sat down long ago." " It certainly tailed off." These are the reproaches you may hear if your ending disappoints the expectations you have aroused.

Remember that everything you have said throughout the speech so far should be capable of being prefaced with " Because," while the ending should be capable of being prefaced with " Therefore." " Because of its policy on education, foreign affairs, atom bomb, Therefore you should support my party." " Because of their extremely interesting lives and works, Therefore you should read the Brontës' poems and novels." " Because of its long and fascinating history, Therefore you should be proud to be part of the woollen textile trade."

Written Notes

To speak without written notes is best for most occasions, but for many speakers, especially at first, it is very difficult. In any case I always take written notes with me on to the platform even if I do not intend to refer to them. Often I keep them in my handbag, or my pocket, or put them on the table under a coffee cup, and never look at them at all; but it is comforting to know that they are there in case of emergency.

At any rate it is sensible to prepare written notes, for a speech once prepared can be used again, sometimes in exactly its original form, sometimes modified to suit the audience or your changing views. When you have delivered the speech once or twice, you perceive its weak points and can improve it. So I make no apology for giving some advice about written notes.

The first question which arises is: should the speech be written out in its entirety, word by word?

There are some occasions when a speech should be thus written out in full, and read to the audience. A paper given to a learned society should be written out and read; a presidential address to a large organisation; a longish speech when royalty or " very important persons " are present; in a word, a speech on any very formal occasion. Such speeches are not performances; they are not meant to *entertain* the audience; the occasion is so important that it would be insulting to risk any lack of smoothness, and words carefully pondered and corrected, as they are in a written text, are sure to be more suitable and dignified than impromptu utterances, however skilled the speaker. Such formal speeches should be typed out very legibly, in duplicate, so that a copy may be handed to the secretary of the organisation for reprint in their transactions, or to the representatives of the press.

But on all less formal occasions, to read a speech is fatal to the audience's enjoyment.

Is it worthwhile, then, to write out the whole speech? For an inexperienced speaker, it is; but it is a habit which should be abandoned as soon as possible. Brief, well arranged notes are the proper method of preparation.

Observe that I say brief notes. Never, never, never take a great sheaf of notes with you on to the platform. This is especially important in England. The English heart sinks when a speaker cheerfully puts his hand into an inner pocket and draws out a thick wad of paper. Slowly, slowly, the wad diminishes as the speaker talks on and each sheet falls; the audience is so fascinated by this slow diminution that it can hardly listen to what the speaker is saying. Hope rises: surely that is the last sheet? No; it is cast aside and there is still another to come. A number, a multiplicity, of objects always leads to counting. Therefore, if you possibly can, get your notes on to a *unit* sheet of some kind. Notes for a very short speech will fit on to a postcard; for a half-hour speech, on to a sheet of notepaper eight inches by five; for a full-length lecture, I often fold a piece of paper ten inches by eight, so that it makes four sides. This gives ample room but still appears only as a unit to the audience. Often the two outside pages suffice for the lecture scheme, and the two inside pages can be used for quotations, statistics, etc. Or a separate small sheet can be used for these. Nobody minds if a speaker picks up a small sheet of paper, reads a quotation or statistic and puts the paper down again; in fact this often gives the audience a feeling of reassurance, a (justified) feeling that you are taking trouble to get your quotations right.

On one small unit of paper, then, write down or type the final form of your notes. I myself have one of those rather orderly, mathematical kind of brains, and I like to have my notes well numbered and divided, with headings underlined (sometimes even in a different colour for the fun of the thing.) Other speakers prefer to let their material flow unrestricted. Which arrangement you choose does not matter so long as it is a definite arrangement with which you are familiar.

Learning the Speech
Now your speech is ready to be learned. Are you to learn the whole thing by heart? Preferably not. Reciting long

screeds you have learned by heart gives a stilted, artificial, insincere effect. At first perhaps you must do so, but try to abandon this habit as soon as you can. But always learn by heart your opening sentence and your concluding sentence. The spoken word differs from the written word, so say these sentences aloud and remodel them into suitable form. You may also have to learn by heart some of those awkward but important " joining " sentences which I mentioned earlier.

The proper way to learn a lecture is to recall to yourself, over and over again, your headings and, in the shortest possible form, the material which belongs to each. Pelmssci, you say to yourself, pelmssci. *Pennines, east, limestone, millstone grit, sheep, streams, coal, iron.* When you know those headings perfectly, go on to the material in each. *Pennines*—where and what they are. *East*—Yorkshire on east side of hills, less rain from Atlantic winds, sheep healthier, no footrot. *Limestone*—North Riding is limestone, has short sweet green grass, good pasturage, water has lime. *Millstone grit*—West Riding is millstone grit; unfertile; grows only heather, bracken, tough grass, this will feed sheep but not good for cattle, water has no lime. So, *Sheep*—in West Riding and nearby in North; Domesday Book, Skipton and Shipley; Kirkstall; Lacy. *Streams*—in millstone grit West Riding innumerable tumbling lime-free streams; water kind to fabric, " tumbling " is source of power later. *Coal and Iron*—deposits fringe millstone grit, helped promote industrial revolution. From these factors: *Wool Textile Trade in West Riding.* Say these headings and sub-headings over and over to yourself until you are thoroughly at home with them and can skip about in them, so that if when you come to make the speech you are interrupted, or forget yourself for a moment, you can retrieve the thread of your argument without difficulty. I myself always " say my headings " at least twice the day before and once on the day of even a familiar speech. Say them just before you fall asleep.

With a new speech or lecture, I then go on to say over the whole thing once aloud in a subdued tone if this is possible, mentally if it is not. This is not only excellent practice but shows up defects and difficulties which need attention. But I do not advise repeating this full-length practice too often; not only is it exhausting but it begins to make the lecture stale. After a little experience you will not need to retain this habit.

I mentioned in chapter two that when I have given a lecture, members of the audience often come up to me and say: " What a talent for speaking you have. How lovely it must be to be able to speak so easily! An hour without a single note! " As you will have seen by now it is not " easy " at all, nor is it a special " talent," but the product of careful preparation and much hard work. I always tell these admirers so. Usually they do not believe me, but you must, if you are to succeed as a speaker.

CHAPTER 4

Chairman's Speeches

Every meeting where a speech of any kind is made has to be presided over by a chairman, and every chairman has to make at least two speeches, as well as calling on the proposer and seconder of the votes of thanks. The office of chairman, and the competent behaviour of chairmen, are therefore two important factors in democracy, and everyone should know how to conduct himself or herself if called upon to take the chair at a public meeting.

Let me make it clear at once, that it is never the chairman's " evening out." The chairman is of secondary importance to the main speaker; he must subdue himself and give the speaker the glory. It is not always possible to ensure that the speaker *looks* more exciting than the chairman, but when two women are concerned it is good when this can be done. Once, for example, my chairman-hostess said to me at teatime: " Excuse me, but I saw a very pretty red dress hanging up in your room. Do you mean to wear red? If so, I won't." Another time my prospective chairman—we both lived in my native town—rang up to inquire what I meant to wear that afternoon. I replied: " Black, with white." " Then I won't," said she. Of course if the occasion is a great one and the chairman is the president, she must flourish in her best; but on more ordinary occasions, a slightly plainer attire than the speaker's will be welcome. The speaker should draw all eyes.

A chairman can be a boon or a bane. A lecture society which I knew suffered so much from their chairmen that

44

they abolished the office. Accordingly, when I went to them to speak, I was chatting comfortably in an ante-room when the secretary, saying " Time now," opened a door and ushered me up a few steps and then closed the door behind me, and I found myself alone on the platform with six or seven hundred people glaring at me. This was an agonising situation, for reasons which will emerge in this chapter; I was very young at the time, and for a moment sheer fright sent every word of my lecture out of my head. Luckily an enormous oak table loomed ahead of me; I walked slowly round it, looking, I hoped, calm and composed; by the time I reached the other side the first sentence had jumped back into my head, and very shakily I began to utter. This was an extreme case, but every speaker has horrendous tales to tell of bad chairmanship. The chairman can in fact make or mar a speech; I come away from meetings usually liking the chairmen, but some-times irritated by them and occasionally quite passionately hating them.

It is really the duty of the secretary of the inviting organisation to attend to the *physical* comfort of the visit-ing speaker; to see that the speaker is met, escorted to the hall and fed, that the microphone, if any, is in proper working order, and that the speaker has all the equipment he requires, including a glass of water. Only once in my life have I needed a glass of water (it wasn't there); but it is always psychologically soothing (and thus preventive of coughs) to have one handy. It is the duty of the secretary; but it is kind and wise of the chairman to inquire whether the speaker has in fact had all his requirements satisfied. If they have been satisfied, the chairman can make some slight private acknowledgment of pleasure to the secret-ary; if they have not been satisfied, the chairman should take steps at once to satisfy them.

It is the chairman's duty to care for the speaker's

mental comfort. Tell the speaker if members are obliged to leave early because of bus-times, professional duties, and so on; otherwise he may feel wounded by their departure. Tell him, *before* he speaks, whether votes of thanks are customary or not; tell him, *before* he speaks, whether questions are customary or not. Tell him whether, after the luncheon, members go up into a gallery, or turn their chairs; tell him whether speeches begin before or after coffee, or whether there is an interval after dinner before the speeches begin, or whether the chairman has announcements to make, and if so when. Tell him, in fact, the whole routine practised by your organisation; to you it is familiar, customary, natural, but to him it will be quite strange, for every organisation (this may surprise you) has its own little quirks which fit its own local conditions. Making a speech is tricky enough; don't upset your speaker additionally by disconcerting him. It is unkind—and besides, you won't get such good service from a ruffled and disconcerted speaker.

Remind the speaker tactfully, of the exact duration of speech required. " As you know, we have to break at two o'clock, because . . ." " I know the Dean told you last night, but you won't forget, will you? Fifty-seven minutes exactly; we're on the air and the conclusion and college song take three minutes." " We like to finish at half past nine, so an hour for the lecture and half an hour for the questions is about right, but arrange it as you like within those limits, of course."

If there are bad acoustics, or any special acoustic characteristics, about your hall, warn the speaker about them. I was once about to go on a platform in the State of Minnesota, to address two thousand university students—it was the fifty-seven minute affair—when a kind man bobbed up from somewhere (I never knew who he was) and said: " Be sure you address the clock, ma'am. There's an echo everywhere else." In spite of considerable tension I managed to address the huge clock which faced me from the front of the gallery, throughout the lecture, except for one half-second when I turned aside; instantly echoes boomed and I lost the audience. What would have happened to me without the intervention of that kind warning, I tremble to think.

Do not talk to the speaker about the subject of his speech just before the meeting. He is trying hard to remember his headings at that time and you will muddle him; or if he is safe on his headings, he is trying to deduce what kind of people he will have in his audience, so as to make the most suitable approach to them. In any case, to talk about the subject beforehand makes it feel stale. If he has told you his best anecdotes, made his best points, both he and you will feel some embarrassment and irritation when he tells them again on the platform. A very brilliant speaker of my acquaintance, badgered over the dinner-table by questions about her subject, exclaimed in anguish: " I don't want to give my lecture twice! " Her chairman-host was shocked, but my heart went out to her.

Of course, speakers vary in their preferences. Some speakers may enjoy a preliminary talk on their subject. But please *ask* them before you embark on it. " I'm longing to talk to you about the Brontës, but perhaps I ought to wait until after the lecture? " The speaker can then reply: " I don't mind at all; go ahead," or: " Well, I should be grateful if we could wait till the lecture is over."

Remember in any case that the speaker is about to use his voice without cessation, for the next hour. Addressing a large audience for an hour or so is hard physical work, even when proper methods of voice-production are used. The speaker is also about to stand on his feet for an hour or so, and this too is hard work. Try to give the speaker a

47

few minutes of quiet, rest and silence, just before the meeting, if you can. He will be grateful.

If possible, show the speaker the auditorium, and ask him where he prefers to stand on the platform. I have spoken from all positions; I like most to stand on the right of the chairman, and least to be boxed in at the centre. The arrangements of furniture—table, chairs, reading-desk if required—should allow the speaker to stand well forward on the platform, so that his voice may carry to the maximum distance, and flowers on the table should not be allowed to impede a clear view of the speaker from all parts of the hall. The chairman should lead the way on to the platform, and indicate to the speaker by gesture where he should sit.

The most important duty of a chairman at a lecture-meeting is to introduce the speaker to the audience. To do this properly, the chairman must know the relevant facts about the speaker. If you are to be chairman for a speaker, you must ascertain what the speaker ought to have said about him, and also what he would like to have said about him. Look him up in *Who's Who*, or in the lecture agency's list, or both; and either write to him or ask him orally if there is anything he would particularly like to be said. It is better to write, so that you know the details in advance and can arrange them in your speech beforehand; but even so it is always well to make a last-minute oral inquiry. Some astonishingly interesting details may emerge thus. He may tell you that he has received a cable that morning announcing that he has been awarded a Nobel prize; or he may tell you that he has landed from Malaya that morning, or he may tell you that he has a particular love for your town because he spent his holidays there as a child once after a severe illness. (Such local details are particularly interesting to the audience.) But if a lecturer ever asks you *not* to mention something about him, please comply with his request; there may be some sorrowful reason for the request, such as a quarrel with his wife, to whom you meant to refer; or it may simply be that he intends to refer to the matter in question himself, and attach other remarks to it.

Whatever you decide to say in your introductory speech, be sure your details are accurate. Everyone hates to have his name mispronounced, or the titles of his books confused, or the position he holds wrongly stated. If you are doubtful on any of these points, ask the speaker before you go on the platform. In my young days I was often announced as " Miss Bennett," even though one or two of my novels bearing my name actually lay on the table in front of the chairman. In any case, I wished to be called by my first name as well as my surname: Phyllis Bentley. Titles, and ranks, are full of pitfalls for the unwary. Not knowing the correct form does not matter in the least; but not to ask the speaker about the correct form is impolite. Lord Sneachey or Lord Thomas Sneachey? Commander Woodman or Commander Robert Woodman or Commander R. V. Woodman? Inspector? Chief Inspector? Superintendent? Captain the Honourable? Lady Jane Grey or Lady Grey? Mrs. Talbot-Jones or Mrs. Jones or Mrs. Catherine Jones? Do, please, ask. John Galsworthy, the kindest and most courteous of men, once in my hearing said quietly to a young chairman after the meeting: " My dear, my name is pronounced Gaulsworthy." The poor girl blushed with shame; but she should have made the necessary inquiry earlier. Personally, when I have to act as chairman, I write the necessary titles, books, decorations, etc., down in full in my notes and read them out. Eloquence is not expected or wanted in a chairman; accuracy is.

The introductory speech by the chairman should not be too short. It is the chairman's duty to settle the audience.

(Remember Abraham Lincoln.) He must battle cheerfully along through the rustling, shuffling, bag-arranging, coat-removing, hat-downing, coin-jingling, acquaintance-nodding, door-closing and late arriving which occur at the beginning of almost every public meeting. By the time he has uttered three or four paragraphs the audience will have settled itself more or less, fixed its eyes on the platform and attuned its ears to long-distance listening. The speaker meanwhile has glanced around, observed the location, age and size of his audience, noticed acoustic difficulties—pillars, archways, galleries and the like—caught his breath and remembered his opening sentence. To give a speaker no time to collect himself after arrival on the platform is sheer cruelty; moreover, unless the audience has had time to have a good look at him before he begins to speak, they will look and not listen for the first few minutes, and then feel annoyed because they have missed his opening remarks. Thus by making a nice little introductory speech and taking all the onus and discomfort of settling the audience upon himself, the chairman has sacrificed himself to the comfort of both speaker and audience. Nobody will thank him, but he has given the meeting a good chance of going well, and virtue must be its own reward.

On the other hand, the chairman's speech must not be too long. Three or four minutes—about five hundred words—is usually enough; five minutes is usually too much. Chairmen who go on too long are agony to the speaker. Once in a Scottish town which shall be nameless my chairman spoke for twenty minutes by the clock. On and on he boomed—uttering, of course, all sorts of things about my subject (more about this crime presently)—while I mentally cut out more and more of my lecture. The audience seethed, and when at last he reached the sentence: " But I must not keep you from our speaker any longer," a storm of resentful clapping arose. If the speaker is famous, the audience wants to hear *him* not the chairman; if he is not famous, a slightly longer than usual introduction is useful, to acquaint the audience with his good points, but too much of this before they have heard him irritates an audience; they feel they are being subjected to pressure, they prefer to judge for themselves.

What is this introduction to contain? First, a sentence of welcome. " I am very happy to welcome here this evening on your behalf . . ."—something of that kind, though very familiar and banal, is true and appropriate. If the occasion is a great one, long anticipated, say so. Then, the speaker's name and experience, accurately related. His general eminence. His authority on his chosen subject. Has he lived in South America for fourteen years? Is he professor of mechanical engineering in the county university? Has she won a gold medal for swimming? Or perhaps written fourteen novels? If so, he or she is entitled to speak on life in South America, or mechanical engineering, or swimming, or fiction. The speaker may have other interests, and if these are especially entertaining they may be mentioned briefly. It isn't really relevant to a lecture on parliamentary procedure that the speaker is a canoe expert, but the fact seems to make him more human. Then, the speaker's special relevance to the present gathering. Is he a native of the town, and you are proud of him? Was he baptised in this church fifty years ago? Is he the pioneer of the movement which the meeting has been called to further? To conclude: call on the speaker to give his speech, giving accurately its title: " It is therefore with very great pleasure that I call upon Commander So-and-So to give us his address on . . ." Do not give the Commander's whole title at this point; a simpler, less formal, though still accurate form sounds warmer.

Are you to say anything about the speaker's subject beyond its title? No, no, and again NO. Probably you know nothing about the subject. That is not a crime; the subject is not your job. Perhaps you know a little about the subject. Good; you are entitled to say so, in a properly modest way. But the speaker is an expert. *After* he has spoken, you will have the opportunity of saying something about the subject; but please, not before. Please, not before! How often have I sat and listened in anguish to my chairman talking about my subject, of which she knew almost nothing; at best taking all my best points, at worst giving them incorrectly. I have watched other speakers undergo the same agony. What are you to do when your chairman voices old ideas, long out of date, which she has painfully gleaned from some unauthentic little volume? It is a misery to have to contradict your chairman, but you cannot honestly leave your audience still believing these exploded theories. I will try to deal with this matter from the speaker's point of view, presently; meanwhile let me once again implore all chairmen: in your introductory speech leave your speaker's subject alone. We all know the story of the chairman who spoke at such length on the speaker's subject that when he at last called on the speaker to give his address, the latter rose and said: " My address is 128 Longworth Avenue. As the chairman has given my lecture, there is nothing to keep me from it. Good night." This story is obviously not true, but it is a useful warning.

It is the chairman's duty to stay on the platform throughout the meeting. Of course you would get a better view of the speaker and enjoy the occasion more, from a seat in the front row. But you have been entrusted with the honourable duty of chairing the meeting, and you must fulfil it and stay in the chair. All kinds of emergencies may arise, with which it is the chairman's duty to deal. Members of the audience may faint; dogs or cats may stroll into the auditorium; the microphone may collapse; doors or windows may blow open. The speaker has no power to deal with these, and no knowledge of local conditions. His only duty is to speak. It is yours to secure the proper and comfortable conduct of the meeting. Beginning a speech while the chairman is scuttling off the platform is excruciatingly uncomfortable for the speaker, and at the end of his speech he feels almost worse. He gazes anxiously towards the chairman, who is slowly clambering up the steps; will she arrive before the applause stops? If not, what is he to do to fill the gap?

It is the chairman's duty to look at the speaker during his speech. If you look at the speaker, the audience will look at the speaker; if you do not, they will do the same. On no account busy yourself with notes or programmes, on no account whisper in the secretary's ear, on no account scan the audience to see if Mrs. Smith is present. I do not mean, of course, that you must glare unceasingly at the wretched speaker; but look at him and listen to him, as though you were genuinely interested, and perhaps you will find that you genuinely are.

Sometimes owing to no fault of his own the speaker is pressed for time; he must leave to catch a train, perhaps, shortly after the conclusion of the meeting. If this is so, tell the secretary and the caterers if any, watch the progress of the meeting carefully and hurry it along. " We have twenty minutes for questions." " Just two more questions, please." But unless you absolutely cannot help it because time is running desperately short, do *not* tell the audience. If you tell an audience that the speaker must leave at 9.30 p.m. sharp, they often feel aggrieved. (" We're paying him, aren't we? ") Even if they don't feel aggrieved, they feel restless. The time is in their minds throughout the speech; they cannot listen to it properly. I have had lectures spoiled in this way, and I eventually decided never to tell the chairman about a time pressure until I had finished my lecture and reached the questions. An exception to this rule arises if the speaker's hurry is due to some very interesting and important engagement. If the speaker has to appear on television at ten, or ask a question in the House of Commons at four, the audience will enjoy a vicarious sense of importance and feel friendly towards the speaker if they know; so tell them.

I ought to have mentioned earlier, but will do so now while we are on the subject of time, that any serious lateness in starting the meeting should be explained to the audience. A few minutes do not matter, but ten minutes or more are not to be passed over. If the reason for the lateness does not concern the speaker, or is not his fault, the chairman should say so. " I'm afraid the twelve o'clock from London was the twelve-thirty, to-day." " Our speaker was on the air until six-twenty." But if the lateness was the speaker's fault, he should apologise for it and explain it himself, as gracefully as possible.

When the speech is over, the chairman must decide when to cut the applause short. A gap here is uncomfortable for the speaker. The chairman should rise at the appropriate moment and utter two or three appreciative sentences. Remember that the proposer and seconder of the vote of thanks have to make appreciative speeches, so do not speak for too long or you will take all their ammunition. If you do not feel appreciative, use some non-committal sentence. " We have heard Commander H.'s interesting and controversial speech." In either case, then say: " Commander H. has agreed to answer questions " or " We have half an hour for questions " or something of that kind, and sit down.

If the subject has been controversial, several questioners may bounce up at once. If so, you are lucky. But some audiences are very slow to begin questions. The larger the audience, the slower people usually are to rise and speak.

So the chairman should always have a question of his own to ask, to fill the gap. " I wonder if I might put a question while members of the audience are collecting their thoughts." " *I* have a question I should like to put, if I may." This is the point where the chairman's knowledge of the speaker's subject, if any, becomes useful and may be expressed.

Do not repeat questions uttered in the body of the hall. I know that this is an old custom, much respected in some parts of the country, but as a speaker I find it exasperating, and so, I suspect, do the questioners. The idea behind it is to make the question audible to the whole audience. But unless you repeat the questioner's words exactly, he is apt to feel aggrieved; while the speaker likes to repeat the question in his own way, perhaps stressing a word or two here and there in preparation for his answer.

If questioners show themselves hostile to the speaker or to each other, it is the chairman's duty to keep order. But the questioners have the right to express their hostility by questions, though not by speeches, and the speaker must answer to the best of his ability. Only if rudeness or disorder is shown, should the chairman interfere. He might perhaps say: " Other questioners seem to be waiting, so shall we leave that point for the moment," if this is true, and if the persistence of some questioners seems to become excessive and contrary to the wish of the meeting in general. But it is the chairman's duty to be impartial, not to protect speaker or questioners from the consequences of what they have said unless disorder threatens. A good friendly argument is proper and enjoyable.

When the time grows late or the speaker grows tired—remember he has put in a hard day's work, travelling, speaking, being on show—the chairman should close the questions. " Commander H. has been very generous in answering our questions . . ." Or: " Unfortunately time is running out . . ." Continue: " So I will ask Mrs. X. to propose a vote of thanks," and when Mrs. X. has finished, call on Mr. Y. to second the vote of thanks.

When Mr. Y. sits down, is the moment when the chairman should express his own appreciation of the speaker. Anything that the proposer and seconder have omitted, the chairman can say now; or if they have said everything needful, he can express his warm agreement. This concluding speech, not more than a couple of minutes in length for the audience are thinking about getting home, should sum up the meeting and leave everyone with a feeling of satisfaction, of something well and truly achieved. The chairman then puts the vote of thanks to the meeting and leads the applause and at its end declares the meeting closed.

If the chairman has enjoyed the speech, or found it interesting, or new, or controversial, now is the time, as the audience file away, to turn to the speaker and say so. To feel that his speech has aroused a genuine interest in his subject is the speaker's great reward. Do not hesitate to admit previous ignorance, or to state some disagreement; the speaker will enjoy a discussion at this point. What breaks his heart is for the chairman to turn away without a word and fall into animated talk with the secretary or other member about some subject entirely unrelated to the evening's programme. If refreshments are served after the lecture, talk to the speaker and bring other people to talk with him; do not leave him alone in a corner disregarded. If you do so, he feels he has been a failure. If he *has* been a failure, talk to him politely but not about his subject. Courtesy will thus be preserved—but he will understand.

CHAPTER 5

Delivering the Speech

On Arrival

Some speakers declare that they do not feel nervous before making a speech, but most speakers arrive with their notes in their pockets and their hearts in their mouths. Personally I have more faith in the nervous speakers than the calm; for if you feel no tension yourself, how can you hope to communicate tension, i.e. excitement, to your hearers? I shall never forget one occasion during the war when I was one of four women who were to broadcast a more or less impromptu discussion to women in France. Three of us were experienced broadcasters and speakers, and as we went down some stairs into the studio, I gave a nervous groan, which was echoed with sympathetic amusement by the other two. The fourth speaker, comparatively quite inexperienced, said pityingly: " Oh, are you nervous? I'm never nervous." At this we three exchanged apprehensive glances, and our apprehensions were all too well justified; our unlucky fourth, terrified when it came to the point and obviously unprepared, at first could not utter a word, then in dismay began to babble incoherently so that the compère was obliged to interrupt. To be nervous simply means that you know a great effort lies before you and are tuning yourself up ready for action. Nervousness is an honourable emotion; it arises from an anxiety not to disappoint your audience. Do not be ashamed, then, of feeling nervous. *But do not on any account show it.*

If you show nervousness it will infect the chairman and

secretary; they will begin to feel doubtful about your competence, will sound uncomfortable and ill at ease. Before you know where you are, the whole audience will be infected, and will begin to think you are a poor speaker and they are in for a poor evening. You will have to fight this down before you can establish yourself—as if that wasn't hard enough already. So keep your nervousness under control; do not fidget, do not snap. If anyone says to you: " Do you feel nervous? " reply with cheerful confidence: " Yes! I always do! " and laugh.

The speaker is entitled to see that proper arrangements for his speaking have been made. If it is possible to have a peep at the hall and platform, keeping unseen, before the meeting begins, that is very useful, but you must only ask for this if you yourself can remain unseen, otherwise your formal appearance later may be an anti-climax. You are entitled to inquire about the microphone, if any; about the blackboard or map or screen or reading desk or exhibits which are necessary; you may even murmur about draughts, and certainly about lighting. Flowers on the table are a very tricky subject; they may seriously obstruct the audience's view and hearing, but all too often are the gift of a member or the carefully prepared structure of a sub-committee. It is almost better to wait till you begin to speak and see if they are a serious obstruction or no; if they are, then say yourself to the chairman, in a voice which the audience hears: " I wonder if I might have these very charming flowers moved to one side? I can't see the audience on my left." I put " very charming " as an example; use what words you like, so long as these are at once appreciative and sincere.

These inquiries and if necessary alterations are perfectly legitimate and will not be resented, particularly if you utter a word or two of appreciation when all is ready. But take it quietly; do not on any account make a fuss.

A chairman told me the other day about a woman speaker who visited a women's luncheon club. She made a tremendous fuss about curtains, lights, draughts, and so on, and then said aloud to the chairman: " I'm told that's the way to impress an audience with one's personality—make a fuss." She had made an impression, certainly, but a strongly unfavourable one. My friend, the officials, and the two or three front rows of the audience who heard her fictitious complaints, all detested her before she uttered a word of her address.

If you are offered a few minutes alone to rest your voice and recall your headings, accept the offer; but don't demand this or you will be thought nervous and uncertain.

Before you go on to the platform, just check the required duration of the speech with the chairman. " It's about an hour you want, isn't it? " " You like to be away by half past nine? "

As I have said in the previous chapter, most speakers have a favourite place in which to stand. If you are asked about this, state your preference frankly. But don't insist on having this special place if another has been allotted to you; there may be all kinds of local precedence involved which makes the granting of it difficult; mayors, trustees, titled persons, donors and the like. If you are allotted an awkward place, treat it as good practice, a challenge. If conditions permit, stand well forward on the platform, so that your voice carries easily.

There are usually a few moments to be spent on the platform before you are called on to speak. May I offer a word of advice on how to sit gracefully when raked by hundreds of eyes? Men look agreeably relaxed and informal with their knees crossed; but only the youngest and most beautiful women do so, and then they offer an appeal not connected with the subject in hand. Keep the knees together. The ankles may be crossed if that feels comfortable, but are best kept side by side. The hands should rest lightly in the lap; to hold a programme or your notes is sometimes helpful. Your eyes may range without fuss over the whole hall, assessing its size and dangers.

Sometimes a horrid panic suddenly seizes one's mind during these last suspenseful moments. "I can't possibly say that," one thinks, and tries to change one's opening words. Don't. Only a very experienced speaker can successfully change his speech at the last moment, and nobody is at their most skilful when in a panic.

On the other hand, some local happening may make a change imperative—a local bereavement or accident may make a joke sound callous. If you have to make a change for such a reason, make it sincerely; the audience will not mind a little stumbling and hesitation if what you are saying is relevant and sincere.

In general, local references are rather tricky unless you know the district well and are absolutely sure of your facts. Names of places may have awkward associations, or be pronounced oddly, or not mean what they appear to mean, and audiences are sometimes as touchy about their towns as about their own names. They can be terribly tired, too, of well known local jokes—in my native town we are sick of hearing people joke about the pronunciation of Golcar and Almondbury, Keighley and Mytholmroyd. Our smile is wan, too, when a speaker yet again quotes the "Hell, Hull and Halifax" saying. Of course a really good new local joke goes down excellently. But check any local reference with a local inhabitant, before your speech.

Beginning the Speech

And now at last the fateful words are sounding: "I call on our speaker, Mr./Miss . . ., to give us his/her address."

The chairman smiles at you and sits down, and the moment of ordeal is here.

Stand up quickly, with a cheerful look, as if you are eager to begin. Never show hesitation or nervousness at this point. Keep your shoulders back, your head up, your chest out, address the back of the room, smile a little, let your voice ring out in cheerful confidence.

Experienced actors, I am told, often speak a little more loudly and slowly than usual for their first sentence or two on stage. I myself do not use this opening slowness on the platform; I have a rather quick personal tempo, and a slow start would inhibit my natural flow of speech; but you may use it if it helps you.

The most important, the absolutely essential point is that your first sentences should be *heard*. Everyone knows the phrase: *Mr. Chairman, Ladies and Gentlemen*—even you in a state of fright cannot forget it. Let it ring! The audience will at once feel cheerful. " We're going to hear, at any rate," they think. You have learned your first sentence by heart, and how glad you are of that now. Say it boldly.

By the way, while speaking, never look at any *one* person, never fix or catch any one person's eyes. If you do so, the person concerned will feel embarrassed and begin to drop his eyes and fidget, while the rest of your audience will feel neglected, not held. Direct your eyes to a point at the back of the hall and at a point so much above your audience's heads that you can keep your own head level or slightly raised. Your eyes will in fact not *see* very much, for they will be as it were turned inward in thought. *Never* look down, *never* bend your head down. If you have to read a quotation, hold the book or paper well up, to avoid having to bend the head, but try to hold the paper so that it is not in front of your mouth and does not impede the sound waves of your voice from reaching the audience.

The Middle of the Speech

Standing up, making your formal address to the audience, uttering your first sentence, is like running along the diving board and diving into the sea; now the splash is over, you surface and begin to swim. From this point onward do not think of yourself at all; think about your subject and your audience. Do not listen to your own voice; think of what you are saying.

Finish your sentences grammatically. This is sometimes difficult, and sometimes you may sound rather ponderous or platitudinous in bringing your sentence to a conclusion. But it is absolutely necessary to do so, if you are ever to become a really good speaker; regard your struggles as good practice. A sentence beginning " when " or " if " or " because " or " whether " is not a main sentence, but just a subordinate clause, it needs a main sentence to complete it. " When " or " if " clauses need a main sentence to follow, beginning with " then " or a word of similar meaning.

> " *When* I see these glorious mountains towering around us, etc., etc., *then* I feel that to ruin their appearance for the sake of a city water supply is base and intolerable."
>
> " *If* wages are to be raised, *then* an increase in price of the product must necessarily follow."

A " because " clause needs a " therefore " main sentence to complete it.

> " *Because* wages are to be raised, it does not *therefore* follow that the price of the product must be increased."

A " whether " clause needs an alternative clause, stated or implied, to balance it, and then a main sentence.

" *Whether* we are to have congested streets and maddening delays, *or* a complete absence of traffic in the centre of the town, is the question I wish to put before you."

" *Whether* we are to have fresh lamb *or* (whether we are to have) frozen, a high standard of edibility must surely be maintained in the original animal."

However, it is not the purpose of this book to give instruction in the use of English; I can only indicate, as I have done above, a few of the more obvious pitfalls.

If you make a mistake at any time, admit it frankly and correct it. " I'm so sorry, I should have said five thousand, not five hundred thousand. Five thousand." " Did I say 1846? I beg your pardon, I meant 1847. Yes, it was in October, 1847, 1847, that *Jane Eyre* was published." It is well to emphasise the correction, so as to stamp it if possible over the wrong statement in people's minds. The audience will not hold such an error against you, though they may joke about it a little among themselves after the lecture. But they will resent, rightly, any mistake made and not corrected; and they will resent furiously any attempt to cover up a mistake, either during the speech or at question time. Though you speak with the tongues of men and of angels for all the rest of the time, the audience will remember only your uncorrected error. " Soon as I heard him say five hundred thousand, I gave him up as a bad job." " She can pretend as much as she likes that she said 1847; she didn't, you know. I mean, if she's inaccurate about *Jane Eyre* you can't trust her at all, can you? " A frank admission of error, on the other hand, often gives the audience more confidence in the speaker. " I liked the way he owned up about that five thousand." " Yes, he seems an honest sort of a chap." " It was just a slip of the tongue, I reckon." I am not suggesting for a moment that you should make an apology for an inexactitude for the unworthy motive of getting on the right side of the audience; I simply tell you that if you behave with rectitude in this matter, you need not fear.

The two great faults of which a speaker must beware are inaudibility and dullness. By careful positioning and voice-practice inaudibility can be avoided. Dullness or interest depends both on the matter and the manner of your speech. We have dealt with the subject-matter in a previous chapter. Now, on the platform, the manner of it becomes extremely important.

Monotony is the road to dullness. A steady, even tone of voice soon becomes boring, and if to this is added a steady, even pace the boredom soon becomes unbearable. An elocution teacher may be able to put some colour, some variation, into your tone; but on the whole you have to do the best you can with the tone of voice you are born with. The speaker with a full, rich voice is lucky; the one with a high, thin tone has a harder task. Your pace of speech, however, is under your conscious control, and can be varied at command. A slow rate for the serious important passages, a light skipping rate for the amusing anecdote, will enliven your speech; a laugh here and there cheers the audience wonderfully. Similarly, use your lower register for the important pronouncement, the higher notes for the more hilarious passages.

Emphasis is useful not only to stress an important point, but to lend variety. So is repetition. But do not use either, too much. An ever-lilting tone and repeated emphasis will not bore the audience, but it will weary and irritate them.

The repetition of certain dull words can be very boring. An experienced journalist of my acquaintance once told me that he very early learned a lesson on this point from his editor. Having proffered a short article to be read by the editor, he stood beside him and awaited his

verdict anxiously. After a while the editor raised his head.
" It's a bit itty," he said.

The word " it " can indeed be confusing as well as boring. Read the following passage:

" It must be remembered that if this diverting of traffic is
to be achieved safely, it must be managed without its becoming too swift or too slow. It will be granted that the
situation has within it the seeds of difficulty; nor can it be
denied that it has aroused resentment amongst many both
qualified and unqualified to judge it."

What does each of these " its " refer to? How irritating
they are!

Other boring words are auxiliary verbs: have, be, will,
shall and so on. They should be avoided if possible, pronounced quickly if not. Good strong transitive verbs,
short nouns, some but not too many well-chosen adjec-
tives, make a speech interesting. For some reason adverbs,
which are very useful in written language, are apt to
sound stilted in speech. An easy conversational style is
very suitable and pleasing except when the subject matter
is emotional and serious; and an occasional slang word or
two, if really relevant, is not amiss. But please, please do
not use slang in the attempt to sound " modern " or clever.
Nothing is more painful than a middle-aged or elderly
person using youthful slang—it is usually out of date and
wrongly applied, in any case.

Obviously, long sentences contain an element of danger.
You or your audience or both may get muddled before
you get through to the end. If the audience appears a little
slumbersome, a few short sharp staccato sentences will
snap them awake.

While I am on the subject of words, may I utter a
caution about the use of foreign words. An audience is

interested by a few foreign words if they are relevant to the subject, but the use of too many will irritate them. Be sure you know how to pronounce these words correctly. The real motive for this care is the belief in truth and accuracy, but there is a lower motive too—you will find there is always at least one member of the audience who knows the language you are quoting! So, be sure to consult some expert, learn the proper pronunciation and practise saying the word to the expert, before the lecture. If this is impossible and you seriously doubt your pronunciation, apologise to your audience for it before you utter the doubtful words. Amusingly enough, I had to do this regularly at one time in a lecture called " Yorkshire and the Novelist." Dialect in the East Riding of Yorkshire differs quite markedly from that in the North and West. A native of the West Riding, I can of course speak that dialect well, but I am often at a loss with the speech of the North and East. So when I had to quote dialect from the novels of Edward Booth, an excellent East Riding novelist, I always apologised in advance; then if sniggers arose during my quotation, I was able to snigger cheerfully too.

If the chairman has said something which you must, for the sake of logical sequence, say again, turn slightly towards him and say: " as you said, Mr. Chairman." This is mere honesty and courtesy on your part, but it will do you no harm. The Chairman will be pleased by this recognition, and perhaps bow and smile slightly, and the audience will enjoy this little exchange. If the chairman has said something which you must correct, do so as politely as possible. " And here, Mr. Chairman, I must disagree, I'm afraid, with your comment on our town's drainage." Leave him out of it altogether if you can. " Here the opinion widely held until recently has been modified by recent research." If he has said something absolutely idiotic, be honest about it, but keep your dis-

agreement light. " Here I'm afraid I must disagree strongly
with you, Mr. Chairman. I hope we shall perhaps be able
to argue it out privately after the lecture."

It is good to sum up what you have said so far, occasionally, especially if the lecture is on an abstract topic. " Well
—so far we have watched the novelist observing life and
taking notes; fictitious characters have formed themselves
in his mind and risen to its conscious levels: he has
investigated and elucidated them, given them a local
habitation and a name. He knows all about these fictitious characters by this time; now he has to make them
known to the reader; he has to put them into words, into
cold print." Such a summary is not only useful in re-
calling what you have said and preparing them for what
you are about to say, but also gives the audience a feeling
of safety and confidence—they are in the hands of a good
steersman who knows where he is and where he is going.

A word here about speaking to foreign audiences. I
have lectured to audiences in Holland and Belgium and to
foreign teachers and students in this country. These may
be infrequent experiences, but to have to welcome foreign
delegations of business or professional men, or groups of
foreign students, is something which might happen to any
of us, so it is worth giving the matter some attention. It
has been my lot also to listen to a good many speeches in
French, Italian and German—of which languages I know
a good deal, something and a little respectively—at
international P.E.N. conferences or writers. My advice is
therefore quite heartfelt. First, don't shout. Far from
making your utterance clearer to foreign listeners, the
boom of a shouting voice blurs the words. Next, speak a
little more slowly than usual; not insultingly slowly, but
in a quiet meditative way. A pause or two occasionally, to
give them time to catch up, is useful. Don't use very idiomatic English, don't use slang. Don't use long involved

sentences; don't use dashes—a great habit of mine, as you see; don't use parentheses (words in brackets). Speak with precision. You would be surprised how difficult it is, when listening to a foreign language, to distinguish the " er " and " um " from the real words. If by any chance your speech has to include weights and measures and lengths, find out in advance the equivalents in the appropriate foreign speech. An inch means to a non-Briton as little as a centimetre means to you. Think how tiresome this Fahrenheit-centigrade business is! In speaking about the Brontës I always refer to their childhood stories and magazines, which were written in incredibly small handwriting in incredibly small home-made booklets, about $2\frac{1}{2}$ inches by one inch in size. Saying this once to a group of French students, I was disappointed to get no reaction ; on a sudden inspiration I continued: " I suppose that would be about six centimetres by two," at the same time indicating the size between my forefinger and thumb. An expression of surprise and interest crossed the students' faces and they sat up, and I had learned my lesson.

Gesture and Stance

This little incident leads me on to the use of gesture while making a speech. An impassioned political speech requires gesture; thump the table and throw out your arms when you feel like it. But do it with all your might. Let your gestures be bold and broad or non-existent. A small, inhibited gesture gives an impression of feebleness and lack of conviction. Women on the whole are not so much given to gesture as men, and this is wise because feminine gestures are apt to be on a small scale. A very good woman speaker I know uses a pretty gesture, throwing out one hand, a kind of expository, this-is-the-way-it-is gesture, and this is agreeable; but she is careful not to use it too much. A gesture too often repeated becomes a bore. As Hamlet said to the players:

> Do not saw the air too much with your hand, thus.
> *Hamlet: Act III*

I think I have mentioned before that if you are speaking to a microphone you must on no account stray away from it; do not either walk away or turn away your head. If you are not speaking into a microphone you are free, of course, and may prowl about the platform if you choose. An occasional prowl is interesting, but too much prowling will get the audience into a fidget. One thing you must never do, and you will think this strange, because it sounds beneficial, but believe me, I am right. If the acoustics of the hall are difficult, and particularly if you are placed (wrongly) in the centre of its long side, you may feel that the wings of the audience on left and right will find it difficult to hear you. You are correct. But do not on any account try to remedy this by turning from one side to the other. If you do, you call attention to the difficulty and thus emphasise it; very soon the three parts of the audience, left, right and centre, will imagine they can only hear you when you are looking towards them, and will feel resentment when you are not. The way to cope with this difficulty is to put more volume into your voice, speak not quite so fast and take more pains with your articulation.

Incidentally, why, oh why, will organisations insist on placing speakers in the middle of the long side of the room? The voice carries in the direction it is given, straight ahead of the speaker; to make oneself heard in a long room is thus infinitely easier than in a broad room. Sometimes when I see where the organisation has placed me—not on a platform; smothered by flowers; masked by a grand piano; with lights overhead so that the audience has to gaze into them or with no light at all so that the audience cannot see the speaker's face; backed by an umbrella stand—my heart sinks almost to despairing point. But such difficulties as these are occupational hazards for the speaker; regard them as a challenge and conquer them.

Always stand to address an audience, however small, unless you have a definite physical disability which prevents easy standing, or the organisation asks you not to stand. If they give you the choice, stand. Believe me, a sitting speaker is *never* so well heard as one who stands. If you sit, the audience cannot see you clearly, for flowery hats and large heads intervene, while the sound of your voice goes out on a wave lower down than it would if you were standing, and encounters the obstacles of human bodies. A few years ago, I heard a superb speech in a large hall ruined by the speaker's sitting position, for the people at the back simply could not hear, and naturally grew restless. A few weeks ago I heard a speech in a smallish room spoiled by the speaker's sitting position; she had a good voice and was heard, but as there was no platform in the room, her face was not continually visible to the middle rows of the audience, who dodged and craned to get a glimpse of it.

Restless Audiences

Several times in the last few pages I have mentioned the audience becoming restless, fidgeting, losing interest, and so on. Restlessness in an audience is worse even than apathy; coughing is the nightmare, the bogey, of the speaker.

Let me say at once that any kind of restlessness, including coughing, is the fault of the speaker. It is true that coughing and rustling are unfortunately infectious, one cough or rustle setting off a score of others; it is true that a bad winter's night, with rain, sleet or fog (snow is not so causal) gives more coughing than a balmy summer's eve, while an overheated hall produces sighs and fidgeting. Nevertheless, if the speaker is sufficiently interesting, no coughing or fidgeting will occur. So, if coughing starts, be more interesting. Bring out your best anecdote. " The Prime Minister said to me last Tuesday . . ." " I was once playing croquet with the poet laureate . . ." This should quell them.

Take no notice of coughing and fidgeting, and show no awareness of them, unless they become really appalling. If they pass the limits of endurance, there is only one thing to do. Suddenly stop speaking. Pause. Look rather severe. Instantly the coughing, fidgeting and so on will stop. After a brief pause, begin speaking again, with a change of pace and tone, and say something new and interesting. The audience, ashamed that their lack of attention has reached the point of discourtesy, will listen intently. A pause of this kind is absolutely effective. But do not pause too long, or the audience will start coughing again, and then it is gone for good. Also never use this pause method more than once in a speech; if you do, the audience will feel resentment. " Treating us like school-children. . . ."

Conclusion of Speech

If the speaker really cares for his subject, he will usually feel some emotion on reaching the end of his speech. Not only his actual words, but his voice, may legitimately express this emotion, so long as it is sincere. A vigorous denunciation (with a thump or two), an impassioned plea (in a moved tone), a deeply felt appreciation, excite and inspire the audience. But anything overdone and insincere will rightly disgust and irritate them. The conclusion of the speech should be its climax, and therefore, as I have said before, beware of starting this climax too soon or too late. To reach suddenly a climactic sentence leaves the audience startled and disconcerted; to go on in a heated excited tone for long minutes makes them recover their critical faculty and become cynical. Worst of all is the speaker who never comes to a conclusion but simply stops and sits.

Applause

Having delivered your speech and seated yourself, you wait in considerable suspense for the applause. If it is poor, do not show any distress or resentment; hold the head high and smile slightly, as if while disagreeing with the audience you understand their point of view. If the applause is good, smile with pleasure. If it is *very* good, stand and murmur " thank you," and give a slight bow. This is the one moment of your stay on the platform when you may properly turn from side to side, to distribute your bows. If you are in doubt as to whether the applause justifies so much acknowledgment, look at your chairman; whether he appears indifferent and inexpectant, or enthusiastic and encouraging, will decide the matter for you. It is ungracious and ungrateful not to acknowledge enthusiastic applause.

I will deal with question time and votes of thanks separately, in later chapters. But to finish as far as possible with the main speaker's part of the evening now, let me mention that it is customary in some organisations to expect a very short concluding speech from the main speaker, after the votes of thanks have been proposed, seconded, put to the meeting and greeted (we hope) with applause. Such a (*very* short, please) speech must inevitably be impromptu, but try to say something more than a general platitudinous expression of thanks, try to show some specific appreciation. If you have enjoyed speaking in this place for some reason, if the audience have been rather especially appreciative of one or two points, if they have listened with great attention and picked up your jokes quickly, if they have given you politically speaking a fair hearing, say so. Speak in an informal, friendly, quiet style. If it is possible to say something sincere in appreciation of the proposer and seconder of the vote of thanks to you, say it. If you are not sure of their names, call them the proposer and the seconder. If you know the name of one of them and not the other, still call them the proposer and the seconder, or the unnamed one will feel hurt. It is not always easy to pick out from their speeches something worth mentioning, something that really pleased you—to pick out points from speeches as they fly requires great concentration in any case—but if you can manage this, it will give great pleasure. A word of thanks to the chairman is also not amiss. If chairman, proposer and seconder have all been merely mediocre, just thank them in general terms " for their kind speeches."

Audiences

A speech is made by the speaker and the audience acting upon each other. The audience is therefore immensely important.

Audiences vary enormously. In Chapter 2 I have urged that the speaker should endeavour to receive some indication of the type of audience he may expect. (I remember once I misread a letter on this point, and found myself addressing a group of women from the faculty of the neighbouring university, instead of a Townswomen's Guild. The interests of the two groups were naturally very different and I had to do some quick thinking.) But even within recognisable categories, audiences vary. Often you can discover the probable character of the audience from the members of the organisation whom you meet in the few minutes between your arrival and mounting the platform. But even so you

may be wrong, for audiences do not always look what they
are. I took the chair once in a West Riding town for a
considerable novelist. The audience was not very large,
and I agree that its members did not look very eager or
colourful, but I could see that the speaker had under-
valued it, and was talking as though they were not keen
readers. I blamed myself for not having explained them
to him before going on to the platform, but there was
nothing I could do at this point. The audience was disappointed and therefore flat. In question time, however,
they showed that they had read every word of that novelist's
work and much else beside; he was cheered and stimulated, things warmed up and we had a delightful evening.

Thus the only reliable way to judge an audience is by its
responses to your speech. Experience will teach you how
to sense what they are feeling. Some audiences laugh
quickly and easily; others sit and glower. Even glowering
is better than apathy, however; oh, those solid rows
looking like sacks of potatoes! How they make the
speaker's heart sink! You must woo them till their faces
brighten.

Never show irritation at the small size of the audience.
It is not the fault of those who are there, after all. If the
chairman expresses regret to you, agree soberly, but say:
" Never mind! Who knows who may be in the audience?
Someone perhaps who will become interested in my
subject and make a really valuable contribution." Then
take a cheerful, friendly, cosy note, a kind of " well, let's
see what we can do together," in your speech and do your
very best, so that everyone present will say to those who
were absent: " What you missed! The best lecture of the
season! " (This may easily lead to another engagement
next season, and however high-minded we are we need not
object to that.)

To handle laughter correctly is an important part of the

speaker's skill. Actors say disparagingly: " She cuts her laughs," of a colleague who proceeds to her next sentence before the laughter at the last sentence has died away. Don't cut your laughs. But worse than cutting them is to wait for them to be prolonged. This annoys the audience. Worst of all is to let the audience see that you are expecting laughter, especially if it does not come. If they laugh, you may laugh with them. After twenty minutes or so of your speech, when you and your audience are in thorough sympathy, you may encourage them to laugh by a smile and a look at the beginning of the story. But don't risk this too soon.

Never show vexation with an audience. If they are not reacting as you wish, they are just as disappointed as you are. If you continue with perfect good temper and self-control, they will respect you, even if reluctantly. If you are in a real howling rage with the audience, tell them so vigorously if you feel you must; it may have a good effect; but remember that if you rage, they are entitled to rage too. At a dinner in honour of a celebrated author which I attended last year, the reception of the speakers was cool at first. The author rose to reply looking furious, and said emphatically, " You're an awful audience. If you don't cheer up, I'm going home." (No prizes are offered for guesses at his identity.) The audience burst into a roar of laughter and the evening was saved. But notice that these two sentences were the only outburst the author allowed himself; he went on at once to make the speech he had prepared. " What I was wanting to say to you was this. . . ." Another sentence of grumble would have chilled the audience, and one more would have roused their anger.

You will comment, perhaps, that many of the recommendations I have made in this chapter merely concern the exercise of ordinary courtesy and good behaviour.

This is true. (Note here, by the way, the useful rhythm variation, the emphasis, conferred by those alternate long and short sentences.) But when a man or woman stands on a platform, alone except for one other person, beneath bright lights, and exposes his or her thoughts for an hour, every quality he or she has is visible as if beneath a magnifying glass; every defect and every virtue leaps to the eye. Honesty, integrity, truthfulness, courtesy, good feeling, self-control, are all even more necessary on a platform than in ordinary life.

CHAPTER 6

Question Time

Asking questions at a public meeting is in itself a form of public speaking, so let me approach the matter first from the questioner's point of view.

I have already mentioned, in Chapter 4, that if questions from the audience seem to be hanging fire, the chairman should fill the gap by asking one himself. If, however, several questioners leap up eagerly as soon as question time begins, the chairman should postpone his own. In general, audiences like the chairman to have the meeting firmly in hand, but not to talk too much; they do not like him to make a barrier between themselves and the speaker.

A person in the audience who wishes to ask the speaker a question should stand up to his full height, and address the *chairman* in a clear ringing tone. " Mr. Chairman, may I (or, I should like to) ask the speaker how the fleece-weight of an Australian merino compares with that of a normal Swaledale ? " The chairman then looks at the speaker, who rises and answers—if he can. Questions should be concise, and neatly expressed. Nothing irritates an audience more than long, dreary, meandering questions of which it is difficult to perceive the point. Such questions are also very unfair to the speaker, who is obliged to try to elucidate them before he can answer them. If the speaker says, as he well may, something such as: " I don't quite follow . . . do you mean . . ." in a puzzled tone, the questioner will feel humiliated; but if he has not made his point clear, this humiliation is his own fault. An attempt to make a speech by a questioner is out of order, and is much resented.

A questioner should in general put only one question at a time, in order to give other questioners their opportunity. The chairman may keep to this rule strictly, and should take care to do so if it is obvious that many other questioners are waiting their turn. But if the questions are related, he may perhaps allow more than one to be put by one person. If you want to put three connected questions, say so. " Mr. Chairman, there are three questions I would like to put, which all have some bearing on each other. First: was the speaker injured when he fell down the cliff? Second: how did they get him up? Third: did he secure the flower he was trying to grasp when the accident happened? " These questions all really relate to one incident, and the chairman may well allow them to be put at the same moment. But unrelated questions are sure not to be allowed in one effort; so pick the most important and put that, and hold the others till later. Of course it is very exasperating to hear a question you have longed to ask, being disallowed by the chairman and put (less well, as you naturally think) by another questioner. But such is life, and one must learn to take public disappointments with unruffled composure.

At political meetings, questions are often hostile to the speaker. This is perfectly legitimate. It is legitimate also to show anger and even passion in your questions. But it is not legitimate to be personally rude. And such is the honourable tradition of British public life that if you become too rude, too offensive, you will turn the majority of the audience against you—not, perhaps, permanently, but for the moment. They will get an uneasy feeling that you are not being fair.

I find it very distasteful when a questioner asks a question merely to score a point against a previous questioner. It is perfectly legitimate to do so. But don't be surprised to receive a crushing rejoinder from the speaker, if you have shown personal bias of this kind. Of course in political meetings, which are essentially part of a nation-wide conflict, all kinds of hostility except the physical are allowed.

To turn to question time from the speaker's point of view.

Question time is always an ordeal to the speaker. Perhaps twenty people will ask questions. These questions are entirely unexpected and unprepared, in the sense that the speaker has no idea what will be asked him. He must rise at once and, without a moment's pause for thought, give the answer in coherent, grammatical, interesting language. He must not be too short, or he will appear to be snubbing the questioner; or too long, or he will bore the audience. The speaker must always be courteous and encouraging to questioners, especially to the nervous and shy. "This is a very interesting point." "I'm glad this has come up." The most maddening kind of question is one which asks something which you have been trying to explain in your speech for the last half hour. But you must remain unruffled; "I find this question very important, but very difficult to answer, because as I tried to indicate in my talk, we have not as yet quite enough data on which to base a conclusion." Or: "I tried to deal with this in my talk and I don't think there is much else I can usefully say. But. . . ." Here repeat very briefly your previous arguments; don't show irritation.

The most difficult kind of question to answer is one of opinion. On a matter of fact you know—or should know—the answer; but when a questioner asks you what you think about Dr. Beeching's railway scheme, or do you think Richard III has been maligned, or do you think Emily Brontë was a better writer than Charlotte, or what do you think about the Prime Minister, then you are in a quandary. To answer such questions of opinion honestly and accurately might easily take you an hour, because you must give reasons for your views. But it is impossible to occupy more than a couple of minutes. Tell the audience your problem. "To answer this question, this very important question, properly would take me an hour. But to answer it shortly: Awful." Or: "Yes." Or: "I rather like him." A jocular note will please the audience and make them see that your answer is not intended to be taken too seriously. Of course, this is the moment for a bright, brief, witty phrase; if you can think of one in time, the evening is made. Don't mourn too much if you think of it too late—make a note; it will come in handy another time.

If the speaker does not know the answer to a question, he must say so frankly. "Frankly, I don't know. I only wish I did." Or: "I have devoted a good deal of time and thought to this question, but I don't yet know the answer." If there is a reason why you do not know the answer, tell the audience. "I do not know, because the statistics for last month are not yet published." "I do not know Emily's capacity as a letter-writer; there is in existence, as far as we know, only one short and formal note to a friend of her sister." The audience does not object to an answer of this kind; indeed it will trust you (rightly) the more for your honest admission; but if you have to say "I do not know" too often, naturally the audience will begin to feel you are not an expert on your subject.

The questioner who thinks he knows better than you on a matter of fact is a real curse; he must be corrected, but it must be done courteously. "Well, I've always been told . . ." he says in a peevish tone, voicing some anti-quated fallacy. You reply in a friendly tone: "That was indeed the view which prevailed in the 1890's, but the later research of which I have been telling you this evening has shown conclusively that it was not in accordance with the facts. This upsetting of a theory by later evidence is a common process, and it is a process by which all research profits."

If a questioner is openly hostile and persists in his hostility, say frankly: "I disagree entirely with the line the questioner is taking, but it is a good thing to have this point brought out and answered."

If the speaker does not know his subject thoroughly, question time can be a misery. The extraordinary things which people ask! Demands rain upon him from all sides, and if he is not careful he begins to lose his nerve. To be saved by the chairman's closure is a relief; but also a humiliation.

But if the speaker knows his subject thoroughly, question time can be a real pleasure to him.

For several reasons. First, because while his speech is very familiar to him, the questions are fresh and therefore interesting and stimulating. Secondly, because questions often enable him to enlarge on a point which he dealt with only briefly in his speech, or which considerations of time forbade him to touch on at all—or which he forgot to touch on! (If so, say so. "I ought to have mentioned this in my lecture" or "I usually mention this in my lecture, but frankly I forgot, and I'm very glad to have the opportunity now of dealing with it.") Thirdly, because thoughtful questions sometimes provide the speaker with new material. A question at a lunchtime speech in Nashville, Tennessee, some twenty-five years ago, provided me with an illustrative anecdote about novelists' handling of characterisation so excellent that I still use it, and a question at a psychologists' seminar in Manchester directed my attention to a point about the childhood writings of the

Brontës which I had not previously perceived. Fourthly, it is really rather fun coping successfully with the challenge of all these questions. It boosts the ego.

If the questions are particularly good, i.e. intelligent and interesting, in your final short speech say so.

CHAPTER 7

Votes of Thanks

One of the most difficult forms of public speaking to perform with credit is the proposing and seconding of votes of thanks.

A vote of thanks must be proposed, seconded and put to the meeting, just like any other resolution.

The first responsibility in this matter rests on the chairman and secretary of the organisation arranging the meeting. It is their duty to see that proper and suitable persons are chosen as proposer and seconder. These should always be contacted before the meeting, so that the chairman is in no doubt as to the person on whom he is to call.

Qualifications

Proper and suitable. These qualifications apply to persons who are interested in the subject of the speech or interested in the speaker. I remember once at a dinner in a large northern city the proposer of the vote of thanks mentioned myself (the speaker) only once and my subject not at all! He began talking about the Pennine Chain, strayed off into his own personal history, stayed there for about a quarter of an hour, and never came back again. The chairman suffered agonies of embarrassment and although I held my head up and looked (I hope) calm, I felt sharply humiliated. When the occasion was over the proposer came up to me, grinning.

" You didn't mind my talking about myself, did you? " he said.

I wanted to hit him, but instead replied coldly:

" Well, yes, I did. I was disappointed."

The grin vanished. " But I didn't know anything about you, you know! " he complained.

At this point the chairman, crimson with embarrassment, intervened.

Everything was wrong about this incident. (It took place many years ago, but I have not forgotten the pain it caused me.) The chairman and/or secretary should not have invited him to propose the vote, or, if he was an important person who deserved and expected the honour, when they discovered he knew nothing about me or my work they should have supplied him with the requisite details. As for the proposer, when invited he should have declined, or if as an important member he wished to take part in the occasion, he should have looked me up; in any case he could have listened to what I said in my speech, and commented on it.

How do you " look up " a person? Your Municipal Library has a copy of *Who's Who*; the library of your local newspaper has cuttings of all local notabilities. The brochure of the lecture agent contains some details. If the speaker has written any books, they will be available in the local Municipal Library; look at one or two. Talk to your acquaintances about the speaker.

Do you say: " All this is far too much trouble to take for a few minutes' vote of thanks speech? "—well, that is your choice. If you wish to be a thoroughly good speaker, you must be prepared to do some work. What right have you to inflict yourself without preparation on an audience?

It is customary in many organisations to invite an important member, or a tried and trusted speaker, or both, to propose the vote of thanks, and an inexperienced, up-and-coming younger member to second it. This is perfectly proper, and a very good way of beginning to train younger speakers. But here too, persons should be chosen for this job who are likely to be interested (whether for or against) in the speaker and what he has to say.

Duration

Local customs vary, and it is always sensible to inquire from chairman or secretary what duration of speech is expected from you; but on the whole you may take it for granted that the proposer should speak for from three to five minutes, and the seconder for about two. If you have something really enthusiastic or interesting to say, of course, you may continue until you have finished saying it. But even so, do not be *too* regardless of time; last buses are looming very large in the audience's minds at this stage of the proceedings; they have been listening for a long time and are anxious to get home. A short, crisp, pointed speech (with a laugh in it, perhaps) will make them really grateful. On great ceremonial occasions, the proposer's and seconder's speeches should be much longer.

To call on the proposer, the Chairman should rise and say:

" I now call on (or I will now ask) Mr. A. to propose a vote of thanks on our behalf to the speaker."

Proposer

The proposer must now rise and say clearly:

" Mr. Chairman, I have much pleasure in proposing this vote of thanks to our speaker. . . ."

If you feel really enthusiastic, you can vary your phraseology:

" I have very great pleasure . . ."

" It is a tremendous pleasure to me . . ."

" It is a great honour and pleasure . . ."

" I knew it would be a pleasure to propose this vote of thanks, for I have heard our speaker before, but I did not realise what a very great pleasure it would be . . ."

If there is any special reason connected with the speaker why you have been chosen as proposer, you may mention it.

"Tom and I were in school together in this town (amusing anecdote) . . . and now here he is, the Right Honourable . . . I'm glad to have this opportunity of congratulating him with all my heart, though I don't agree with him politically. . . ."

"Believe it or not, it was I who taught Commander H. to climb. . . ."

"It was I who first proposed Mrs. . . . as a member of our local committee. . . ."

"I knew her when . . ."

"I have been a fly-fisher for twenty years. . . ."

"My early association with our speaker was not very creditable to me, I'm afraid, for I used to steal the apples in her father's garden. In chasing me off, she showed all that energy and intelligent foresight which her speech tonight has revealed so admirably. . . ."

"My only qualification for this pleasant task, but I believe it to be a real one, is that I have attended the first night of every one of our speaker's plays. . . ."

If you have no special connection with the speaker or his subject, don't mention the matter. Never, never, NEVER say: "I don't know why I have been asked to propose this vote of thanks." You mean it modestly, I know; but don't you see, it is an insult to the speaker? It implies that the chairman sought round madly but could not find anybody who wanted to propose the vote of thanks so in despair he asked you! If you really feel inadequate to the occasion and feel you simply must say so, use some such words as these:

> " I feel it is an honour that I have not deserved, to propose this vote of thanks, but I have enjoyed the lecture so very thoroughly that I take courage . . ."

> " Before the lecture I knew very little, I must admit, of the speaker's subject, but for that very reason I have pro-fited enormously by what he has told us. . . ."

Notice that the important word in these remarks is " but." Pass on as quickly as possible from your de-preciation of yourself to your appreciation of the speaker. You must imply—if it is true—that in spite of your own disabilities you have enjoyed the lecture enormously.

Never say: " It was very good of the speaker to come " unless (1) exceptional circumstances have made this true, or (2) there is absolutely nothing else to say. If your district is remote and your audience small, or if the speaker has waived his fee, or if the speaker has at very short notice filled a gap, then you may say this very warmly, for long journeys can be very fatiguing, lectures require preparation, to miss a day's work and receive no pay is a real sacrifice and to be reft suddenly away from home can be inconvenient. But if none of these con-ditions operate and the speaker is being properly paid, he is not being " good " to come and speak to you, he is merely doing his job. My heart always sinks when a proposer begins in this way; it usually means that he has not been able to think of anything else to say. This is in itself an adverse comment on either the proposer's intelligence or your own; and after a day's travel, a couple of hours on show, an hour's lecture and half an hour's questions, a speaker is often too tired to feel self-confident.

What should a proposer say, to give real pleasure to the speaker?

If possible he should comment on both the *matter* and the *manner* of the speech.

To make any relevant and sensible comment on the matter of the speech, the proposer must attend in a most concentrated way throughout, and to jot down a few notes is very useful. Thus I myself am always rather disappointed when asked to propose the vote of thanks, because to listen in this different way, and to make notes, takes the edge from my enjoyment. Besides, I feel nervous as to whether I shall do the speaker justice when the time comes. But as the speaker goes along, I usually become keenly interested in the necessary way, i.e. I perceive points on which I should like to comment.

It is good to think of a general comment on the speech as a whole, and also if possible say something about a few of these specific points.

For example, on the matter in general:

" This story of high adventure has really thrilled me and I'm sure all of us . . ."

" I had no real knowledge of the work of probation officers before this evening; now thanks to our speaker I feel I understand what they are trying to do, and I regard their work with great respect. . . ."

" Our speaker has made this complex situation clear to us. . . ."

" What a tragic but fascinating life-story the speaker has told us! "

" We have heard a clear and forthright exposition of the principles and policy of the . . . Party."

" He has brought this beautiful land vividly before us."

On specific points in the matter:

" I thought her analysis of the structure of *Wuthering Heights* particularly illuminating."

" I had never realised before, the antiquity of our Parish Church. Nor had I realised what a stormy history we had in this town in the seventeenth century."

" What I enjoyed most was his story of the chimpanzee."

" I shall never forget those last few hundred yards to the summit."

" His plain speaking about nuclear warfare was painful but necessary."

The speaker is very glad indeed to hear that the purpose of his speech has been well achieved and his anecdotes appreciated. But, such is human nature, he is even more delighted to have the *manner* of his speech praised.

" The acoustics of this hall have not always proved easy for our speakers, as we have sometimes found to our cost, but I think everyone here to-night has heard every word the speaker had to say."

" What a wonderful delivery! An hour and a quarter without a single note! Never at a loss for a word! "

" Such a pleasure to hear such beautiful English . . ."

" The alternation of light and shade, of the poignant and the humorous . . ."

" The speaker has held us enthralled . . ."

" Sparkling . . ."

" Brilliant . . ."

" Convincing . . ."

" We felt at home with the speaker from the start, and he has not betrayed our trust."

This is the kind of comment which makes public speaking a joy to the speaker.

But suppose you don't feel inclined to make this sort of comment? Suppose the speaker has been inaudible, feeble, stumbling? Votes of thanks must be sincere, not only for the sake of truth and honesty—though these are over-riding considerations—but also because false praise of a bad speaker is so very unfair to a good speaker. If you are fulsome about the failure, what are you to say next week about the success? Never say anything you don't mean. Don't say you have pleasure in proposing the vote, if you have no pleasure in it; avoid the phrase and say instead something like:

" In proposing this vote of thanks, Mr. Chairman . . ."

Even the worst speaker usually says one good thing; pick on that.

" In proposing this vote of thanks, Mr. Chairman, may I say that I gained very useful information from the speaker's description of his half-hour with President Nasser. I thought that was interesting, because . . ."

If you find yourself in the really awkward position of disagreeing strongly with the speaker's opinions or facts, you must say so. But this must be done courteously and urbanely.

"I'm sorry to say, Mr. Chairman, that I disagree entirely with the speaker's views on unilateralism, and I hope our Party never comes to adopt his policy. Nevertheless, our speaker has come before us and declared his thoughts honestly and openly, and for that I am prepared to propose a vote of thanks."

"I'm sorry to say, Mr. Chairman, that my views on Charlotte Brontë's feminism are contrary to the speaker's views, which I believe to be utterly contrary to the evidence. I should like to argue it all out with her. But she has put her views very clearly, and by that clearness has stimulated us all to give more thought to the matter; for that I thank her."

If the speaker's performance has been really too awful for words, don't use any words. Simply rise and say in a level inexpressive voice:

"Mr. Chairman, I propose that our thanks be given to the speaker."

Say no more, and sit down.

It is customary to conclude a speech proposing a vote of thanks by repeating the purpose of the speech.

"And therefore, Mr. Chairman, I have very great pleasure in proposing that our best thanks be given to the speaker."

"And so, Mr. Chairman, it is with very great pleasure indeed that I propose this vote of thanks to Commander H."

When the proposer has concluded, the chairman rises and says:

"Thank you. I now call on Miss Z. to second the vote."

Seconder

Poor Miss Z! If it mars one's enjoyment of a speech to have to propose the vote of thanks, to have to second this vote ruins it. For what is she to say? Miss Z. has no doubt conscientiously noted down several points in the speech, but on all of these the proposer has probably commented. The proposer has probably been appreciative about the speaker's general record, and has commended both his matter and his manner. So what is left?

Only Miss Z.'s personal feelings about the speaker and the speech.

If Miss Z. feels that she has really almost nothing left to say, let her begin like this:

"I have great pleasure in seconding the vote of thanks so ably proposed by Mr. A. I agree most warmly with everything he has said."

Then she really must try to find something all her own, something personal, something different from Mr. A. to say. For example, on the *matter* of the speech:

"May I just say that I personally liked the story about the parrot best, because . . ."

"Aside from the excitement of the ascent which Mr. A. mentioned, I was keenly interested in all the preparations. I had no idea—I think most of us had no idea—of the immense amount of work which had to be done beforehand . . ."

" The story of the tiny books fascinated me . . ."

As to the *manner* of the speech, let her say something different from Mr. A. if possible, but if it is not possible, let her express her whole-hearted agreement:

" I too was enthralled by the speaker's wonderful flow of language . . ."

If Miss Z. can second a vote of thanks by saying entirely different things from the proposer, she is potentially a good speaker, for she can think quickly and express her thoughts coherently.

Preparation
As you have no doubt observed, I have not yet recommended any preparation of their speeches for the proposer and seconder of votes of thanks.

I can't help telling an amusing anecdote here. After a hard day's travel I was once sitting alone in the parlour of a convent boarding school in New York state, enjoying a refreshment of milk and biscuits, when I heard a disembodied voice saying:

" It is with very great pleasure, Miss Bentley, that I rise to thank you on behalf of the School for your fascinating lecture on character in fiction. It will help us, I am sure . . ."

I turned cold and the nape of my neck prickled. Had I gone mad? What time was it? Had I already given my lecture? Had I been in a coma? To my immense relief I next heard:

" Say it once more, my child."

What I had heard was the head girl rehearsing her vote of thanks in the next room to one of the nuns. To know in advance what she was going to say damped my enthusiasm a good deal—for however hard I tried I could earn no higher praise. Something of the same feeling makes the speaker sigh as he listens to the stilted utterance of a pre-packed tribute.

Much preparation by votes of thanks speakers is not to be recommended. Their first and last sentences are already settled. Preparation in the general sense, of making themselves acquainted with the achievements and character of the speaker, is certainly desirable, but to frame these speeches too carefully gives them a stilted, amateur air. Besides, these speeches should refer to the speech just delivered and therefore cannot be prepared in advance. Nothing is flatter and more disappointing to speaker, chairman and audience than proposing and seconding of votes of thanks which do not refer, plainly and clearly, to the speech which has just been heard. If you have something not referring to that speech, but only to the speaker, which you very much wish to say, admit openly that it is not quite relevant but you think it will be interesting.

" I have long wanted the opportunity, Mr. Chairman, and I hope you will forgive me if I take it now, to offer our speaker my personal thanks for something which he did three years ago . . ."

" I don't know if I am in order in saying this, Mr. Chairman, but I hope you will allow me to offer our speaker my warmest appreciation for his new book, which I was reading last night and until three o'clock this morning . . ."

The chairman and the audience will forgive you, and be interested, provided you don't take too long about it and come back quickly to the real matter in hand, i.e. the speaker's speech. The speaker will be delighted.

The chairman must now put the vote of thanks to the meeting.

" I will put the vote of thanks to the meeting. Those in favour ? "

Hands will be raised. " Those against? " is a mere formality and can usually be omitted. The chairman then says:

" Shall we show our appreciation in the usual way ? "

Applause then follows—or at least we hope so.

As I have mentioned in previous chapters, the speaker sometimes says a few final words at this point. If he (or she) will remember his own difficulties when he has been invited to propose or second a vote of thanks on some earlier occasion, he will utter a kindly commendation of Mr. A. and young Miss Z.

Vote to Chairman

I ought to mention here that sometimes the chairman is included in the vote of thanks. This is a rather awkward custom for several reasons. After enthusing about the speaker, the proposer and seconder have to become prosaic —for although the chairman's services have been both necessary and substantial, they are not very obvious; indeed the better the chairman the less obvious his services will be.

" May I also thank the chairman for his kind services this evening? "

This is about as far as you can go without seeming effusive—unless, indeed, the meeting has been political and stormy, in which case the chairman deserves a vote of thanks all to himself, I feel.

Another awkwardness of this custom is that if the chairman is included in the vote of thanks, he cannot put the vote to the meeting. The proposer of the vote must therefore put it, turning round to face the audience. Somehow this always seems either to leave the chairman high or dry, or diminish the speaker, or both; the applause is never as enthusiastic when the vote of thanks is dealt with in this way. Personally, speaking as one who often takes the chair, I know that it is not the chairman's evening out, and I am quite content to go home unthanked, particularly if the speaker gives me a kind word in his last remarks.

CHAPTER 8

Illustrated Lectures

The day of the full-scale " Illustrated lecture " with a huge screen, a lantern, a paid assistant and glass slides, is over. But the day of the amateur and educational showing of transparencies is very much with us, and will increase as the interest in photography as a hobby grows. It is a great pleasure to make one's own coloured pictures of one's own holiday, and to show them later to one's friends; while the use of transparencies is obviously the coming way of teaching geography and art. Moreover, Women's Institutes, Townswomen's Guilds and other similar groups form a continuing audience for the illustrated travelogue, and small groups devoted to painting, sculpture, gardening, archaeology, history or literature and so on, are interested in relevant illustrations.

Such " transparency talks " can be a rich delight to the audience, or an unmitigated bore; I have had both experiences as a member of the audience, and have given a talk of this kind myself which was a muddled failure, so I speak from experience.

Equipment

A word first about your equipment: projector, screen and transparencies. Projectors can of course be of different powers, and while the projector you use at home in a small room may be satisfactory there, it may be inadequate for the village hall where a 500 watt bulb may be needed. Conversely, a hall type projector may give too dazzling a light for a small room. On this point you need professional advice. Be sure to take with you to the talk an adaptor for your projector plug, and a spare bulb—bulbs are apt to " go " at the moment when you put them in.

Do try to see the hall or room you are going to talk in, before the occasion, and decide where the projector and screen should be placed. This is particularly necessary in an ordinary room where there is no settled indication—by benches, platform, etc.—as to placing. The audience find it tedious to wait while projector and screen are assembled and placed, particularly as nervous haste often causes mistakes and delays. Strings tie themselves into knots, screws refuse to screw, screens roll themselves up, tripods collapse, under nervous fingers. Still more irritating to a small audience of this kind is the discovery that the screen has been placed at the wrong end of the room so that chairs have to be reversed. The mingling of sardonic enjoyment and exasperated compassion which these mishaps cause in your spectators is not conducive to the proper mood for " Us in Albania " or " Modern Abstract Sculpture." Competent technique, on the other hand, commands (at least initially) respect.

You are fortunate if you have a friend to accompany you who knows your projector and screen, or if you can discover in the caretaker or among the audience someone who is familiar with similar equipment. Helpers unfamiliar with the problem are useless and even dangerous.

Transparencies

Transparencies are part of your equipment; regarded as equipment, it is your duty to learn how to handle them. How many, many transparencies are put in for the first time upside down! Why this should be so funny I do not quite know, but St. Paul's standing on its dome always raises a laugh, and with modern abstract art transparencies a doubt may well be left in the spectator's mind as to

which *is* the right way up and whether you really know it.
So make sure that all your transparencies are right way up
in their box before you leave home. Transparencies should
be kept in a compartmented box made for the purpose;
there are plenty of inexpensive slide-boxes of this kind,
made in wood or plastic, to be found in the shops. Transparencies should *not* be stacked on the table in a pile,
where a mere touch will upset them. You retrieve them
hurriedly, thus throwing them out of order and disordering
your lecture. I am told that there can now be obtained
long frames to hold several transparencies which move
along through the projector at the touch of a switch. I
have not seen these myself, but they will certainly help the
lecturer.

Your transparencies are more than mere equipment; for
they are the substance, the material, of your lecture.
While thinking about this chapter the other day, I said to
an artist who gives lectures, illustrated by transparencies,
on the history of art to school upper forms, W.E.A.
classes and so on: " What is the most important point in
the preparation of your lectures? " She replied at once:
" The order of the slides." She went on to explain that in
such lectures one required an introduction, a theme
developed, and a conclusion. In a word, the preparation
of an illustrated talk requires exactly the same procedure
as that outlined for unillustrated talks in Chapter 3, the
only difference being that the transparencies serve as headings.

Theme

The first thing to do, then, for even the simplest family
talk, is to decide on your theme, your angle of approach.
You have some excellent transparencies taken while on
holiday last year in Venice. Is your theme " Our Holiday "
or " Beautiful Venice "? You took some pictures while at a

Conference in Edinburgh. Is your theme " The P.E.N. Conference," or is it " Me in Edinburgh," or is it " Beautiful Edinburgh? " The same slides will probably serve for all three, but only if they are differently arranged, and subjected to a few additions and subtractions. The story thread must be maintained all through.

If your theme is " Our Holiday," for example, you may properly begin with slides showing the family packing themselves into car or train or place; but if your theme is " Beautiful Venice," obviously your first slides should show the railway station at Venice, with the astonishing water at the foot of the steps. " Me in Edinburgh " begins with you at the Waverley Station; " Beautiful Edinburgh " with a distant view of the city; " The P.E.N. Conference in Edinburgh " with groups of P.E.N. personalities, Edinburgh landscapes as background.

Selection of Pictures

My artist friend tells me she has found it wise, when planning the "travelogue " talks she occasionally gives, not to be too strict in insisting that the transparencies should be all one's own. Of course this must be announced to the audience. " I took these myself except for three or four; I'll tell you which they are as we go along." But so long as it is told the truth, the audience does not in the least mind that you bought a few transparencies in order to improve the sequence; the more thoughtful will be interested to see that the colour of the sea, the trees, the snow, the Doges' Palace, is the same in the bought transparencies and yours. A plane landing at an airport, an aerial view of Rome, a distant view of Florence from the Piazzale Michelangelo, of Edinburgh from Arthur's Seat, of Notre Dame from the Seine—these are beyond the ordinary amateur's skill; but they make glorious opening pictures. Similarly a sunset over Venice makes a superb conclusion. It is better to sacrifice your pride a little and give the audience the pleasure of seeing these fine professional pictures than to be adamant about the slogan " all my own work."

In arranging the pictures to illustrate your theme, you will find the easiest and best type of arrangement to be either chronological or geographical—that is, either by time or place. Keep strictly to whichever you choose. Unless you make a plan and keep to it, we shall hear from you things of this kind: " Oh, this is us at A. . . . We were coming back from B . . . Or were we going there? We went twice, you know. . . . Well, anyway B was a lovely place; there's a picture of it somewhere. But this is A."

Make a plan, arrange your pictures, write them down in order in a list, and keep the list in your hand throughout your talk. The light spilling from the projector at the sides should be enough for you to read by; if you fear it will not, you must write your list in black Indian ink.

Some users of transparencies like to print the name of each picture on the appropriate groove in the transparency box. This might be a good method, but all too often more transparencies are added later in the middle of the series and confusion results.

Following a chronological plan involves dating your pictures accurately, and listing their place accurately, whether you are aiming at a light-hearted travelogue or a serious lecture.

My artist friend tells me that her audiences like some " human interest " in a transparency talk, whether its subject is gardens or Greek sculpture. Personally, I am allergic to " human interest " in serious talks about other matters, and still more so to animal interest; a cat in the act of dashing across the screen, or somebody drinking a glass of lemonade, tend to spoil my enjoyment of the landscape; but I know I am in the minority here and I advise you to follow her advice.

Preparation of Text

The opening and closing sentences of a transparency talk should be written carefully and learned by heart. The middle of the talk should not be learned by heart—after all, you have the pictures there before you on the screen to remind you of what to talk about. But do make up your mind beforehand on what you mean to say. Don't let us have this sort of thing:

" Oh yes, this is the leaning tower of Pisa. As you see, it leans. Now what was I going to say about it? Oh, I remember . . ."

One last word of advice. Whatever picture appears on the screen, talk about that picture, and that picture only, as long as it is on the screen, and stop talking about it when it disappears. If you are putting the slides into the projector yourself, you can control the duration of the appearance of a picture yourself; if a helpful friend or assistant is putting the slides in for you, a signal is necessary. Arrange this before your talk starts.

CHAPTER 9

Speeches at Minor Functions

Though we are not all public speakers in a professional or important-amateur sense, we nearly all have to make short speeches at one time or another, at minor functions. We have to propose toasts, open bazaars, make presentations, give prizes. These affairs are the very stuff of life; do not despise them. To some of the people present they are terrific occasions, which they will remember all their lives. My wedding day; the day I won the mathematics prize—it started my career; my retirement day when the firm gave me my gold watch; the day they gave the dinner in my honour. If you are taking part in such a function, therefore, you owe it to your fellow human-beings to do your very best to make the affair decorous, pleasant and memorable. Don't send them home feeling flat or disappointed; don't send them home with a little uncomfortable thorn in their breast where all should be warmth and happiness.

After-dinner Speeches

Let us take after-dinner speeches first.

The tradition of after-dinner speeches is that they should be humorous, and this should to some extent be observed; but let me warn you once again that women are not so devoted to humour as are men. The *relevant* funny story is enjoyed by all; but mere facetiousness receives a cold welcome from my sex. Also, no audience can bear stale jokes.

Please believe that any joke you have heard on television or radio is from that very fact stale. I learned this lesson in a very painful way. I was to reply to a toast at a dinner of Yorkshiremen in a city I will not name. I wished to make some points about Yorkshire, which I proposed to illustrate by a few amusing anecdotes. A week or two earlier I had used some of these anecdotes in a television interview, but I mistakenly thought this would not matter. The proposer of the toast arose, spoke of me (very agreeably) as a Yorkshire novelist, and *told all my anecdotes*, which she had seen me telling on television. My speech fell in ruins; I had to think of new points and new anecdotes, in about three minutes. I have never spoken worse in my life. The only way to ensure that your anecdotes are really fresh is to tell only stories which happened to you personally, which you have not told to anyone before. An anecdote stale in one's native town used to be fresh in a distant county; it may still be so only if it is your own anecdote, not one borrowed from another source.

Here is an anecdote about an anecdote. A well-known male author was once about to take the chair for a well-known female author. He asked her how she meant to begin her speech, and trustingly she told him her opening anecdote. The abominable man for a joke told this anecdote in his introductory remarks. The speaker arose with a delightful smile and fury in her heart, and began: " Your chairman has told you the story with which I meant to begin my talk. All I can do is tell it again! " With great aplomb and a better wit than the chairman, she did so; she was roundly applauded, and the chairman, who later told me this story, admitted that she had scored. But what a risk to have to take! The moral of this is: keep your anecdotes to yourself privately if you mean to tell them publicly.

The first toast at any dinner in Great Britain or the

Commonwealth is, of course: THE QUEEN. No speech should ever be made on this toast, which is always proposed by the chairman, and smoking is not allowed until it has been drunk, when permission is given by the chairman.

The other speeches at a dinner are arranged into what is called a " toast list," and this list is usually printed on the menu. It will look something like this:

Toast: GLEBESHIRE.
     Proposed by: Councillor P. Oxmarsh, O.B.E.
     Reply: The Right Hon. Denis Ydom, M.P., C.P.

Toast: THE GLEBESHIRE COUNTY CRICKET CLUB.
     Proposed by: Mr. T. F. Hones, J.P.
     Reply: Mr. J. M. Ardent, Captain of the team.

or like this:

Toasts

THE FEDERATION OF UNIVERSITY WOMEN.
     Proposed by: Mrs. J. M. Smith, B.A.
     Reply: Miss G. F. Jones, B.A., D.Litt., C.B.E.

THE ANNOTSFIELD BRANCH OF THE F.U.W.
     Proposed by: the Chairman of the Hudley Branch,
                    Miss M. Abraham, M.A.
     Reply: the Chairman of the Annotsfield Branch,
                    Mrs. T. A. Golightly, M.Sc., M.D.

THE TOWN OF ANNOTSFIELD.
     Proposed by: Miss F. Clayton, B.A.
     Reply: His Worship the Mayor of Annotsfield.

Three toasts is a reasonable number for an ordinary

provincial dinner, but I have known an occasion when there were five. (I was to reply for the fifth.)

You will have seen at once that the speakers who reply are the most important and interesting—the main speakers of the evening. The most important speaker usually replies to the first toast; he is the biggest celebrity the organisation can catch, often a man or woman from the capital headquarters of the organisation; always an important figure in some activity relative to the organisation's work. The organisation puts up the best speaker amongst their faithful and useful workers, to propose this main toast.

There are therefore two kinds of speeches to be made at dinners: the proposal of the toast and the reply to it.

At very formal dinners a toast-master is employed. This functionary, very formally attired—usually in a red dress-coat—stands behind the chairman with a mallet in his hand. It is his duty to announce the speakers. At a word from the chairman he steps forward, strikes with his mallet on the table (usually three times) and says in a strong resonant tone:

" My lords, ladies and gentlemen (or whatever form of description the assembly requires), pray silence for Councillor Percy Oxmarsh, O.B.E., who will propose the toast of Glebeshire."

At less formal dinners, the chairman will call upon the Councillor in the usual way. After a few opening remarks about the organisation—" this is our 37th annual dinner, a tribute in itself to the vigour, vitality, and usefulness of our society . . ." or " This is our first dinner, but we hope the experiment may be successful and the dinner become a regular annual event . . ."—he says: " I will now call upon

Councillor Percy Oxmarsh, O.B.E., to propose the toast of Glebeshire. Councillor Oxmarsh."

The diners give a welcoming round of applause, and Councillor Percy then rises and begins his speech. He begins with the proper form of address:

" Mr. Chairman, my lords, ladies and gentlemen . . ."

If Councillor Oxmarsh is clever, he will repeat exactly what the toast-master or the chairman said in this matter, because then he is sure to be correct.

The customary opening for the proposal of a toast is:

" It is a great pleasure to me to propose this toast. . . ."

The rest of the speech is devoted to explaining *why* it is a pleasure. Of course if you have a really superb relevant anecdote for your opening, use that; but it must be really relevant and really superb.

A speech proposing a toast must be planned thoroughly beforehand. From five to ten minutes is usually ample for a toast—be sure you ask the secretary or chairman about this duration, well in advance—and in such a short time you cannot afford to flounder or hesitate. It is useful, as always, to have a few main headings in mind.

" It is a great pleasure to me to propose this toast—for three main reasons."

When you have stated your reasons as convincingly and entertainingly as you can, you take hold of your glass and say:

" I therefore ask you to rise, and drink with me the toast of Glebeshire, coupled with the name of the Right Honourable Denis Ydom, M.P., C.P."

The old-fashioned form of this is: " I therefore ask you to be upstanding, and drink with me, etc." Personally I rather like the flavour of " be upstanding," but you must judge from the mood of your audience whether it will go down well or not.

Notice the " coupled with the name of " phrase. The name of the person who is to reply to the toast is always thus coupled with it, and his (or her) name should be given formally, in full, with all the distinctions he (or she) has earned, attached to it.

The company then rise, and murmuring: " Glebeshire! Denis Ydom! " drink the toast. They then sit, and applaud your speech and the responder.

If the toast is made to a person, of course the phrase " coupled with the name of " is omitted; the proposer simply asks the audience " to rise and drink to the health of the Right Honourable Denis Ydom, M.P., C.P."

At a very formal, large dinner, the proposal of a toast may be allotted more time than I have suggested. But with each toast the duration should shorten, and by the time the last toast on the list is reached only a very short, crisp speech is endurable. I advise you not only to ascertain the proposed duration of your speech, the names and honours of the responder, and the place in the list of your toast, before the day of the dinner, but also to look at the toast list and check all these details as early as possible when you reach the reception at the function. People fall ill or are called abroad, substitutes have to be found, the harassed secretary has not had time to tell you of the change, though he certainly ought to have done so; you may find your toast has whizzed up or down the list, and that the responder is no longer the Mayor but a lady missionary from China.

Turning now to the response to the toast, I find very little that is new to say, for a speech of this kind can be of almost any style and content, depending on the nature of the occasion. I have heard serious declarations of new policy, accounts of previous work, pleas for funds, statements of principles, light-hearted jests, vistas of sentiment, tributes to great figures, and short lectures on relevant topical subjects, all delivered with perfect suitability as after-dinner speeches.

This diversity is indeed one of the reasons why I myself am never very happy when asked to make such a speech; the range of choice is so wide, one simply does not know what line to choose. (One says to the secretary: " What would you like me to talk *about*? " The secretary replies cheerfully: " Anything you like.") The two great criteria to apply when deciding what line to choose for an after-dinner speech are of course the familiar ones: What is the audience interested in? What special contribution can I personally make to that subject? But the difficulty of choice is increased by the fact that at dinners of this kind male members of the organisation are often accompanied by their wives, or if the members are female, by their husbands, so that the audience is decidedly heterogeneous. No wonder that humorous anecdotes are seized on with relief, as common ground!

When you have chosen your line, prepare your speech in the ordinary way, learning the opening and concluding sentences by heart, planning your headings and devoting special thought to your examples, your illustrative anecdotes. The response to the main toast of the evening should occupy from twenty to thirty minutes, depending on how many other toasts there are on the list. At a very large formal dinner, you may perhaps allow yourself thirty minutes, if you have checked this in advance with the secretary or chairman.

Incidentally, secretaries without much experience of dinners are apt to be rather unreliable about the duration of speeches. " Oh, we shall want more than *that*! " they exclaim enthusiastically when you suggest twenty minutes. It is wise to ask them at what hour they expect the function to conclude; then do a little private arithmetic about the number of toasts to follow. In any case, keep your eye on the clock. If the affair is running to time, you may expand; but it usually doesn't! It is very difficult to judge at a dinner how long to continue speaking once you have risen to your feet, for the audience, lounging comfortably and smoking after a heavy meal, often look half asleep and inattentive, so that it is difficult to tell whether they are listening or not. A joke will wake them up—if it doesn't, draw to a rapid close. It is better that people should grumble: " He didn't go on long enough," than that they should yawn: " I thought he was never going to stop." The important point is that your address should be meaty, full of interest from start to finish.

If your name occurs down towards the end of the toast list and the hour has grown late before your turn comes, don't waste time in moaning about this to the audience. If you mention the hour to them, they will all look at the clock or at their wrist-watches; so leave the time alone. Just spring to your feet—no notes visible, *please*—and rapidly and amusingly and firmly and cheerfully put one strong clear point to them.

As you will have seen from this account of the proceedings, a toast does not need to be seconded or voted upon. The proposer simply asks those present to rise and drink the health of whatever it is, coupled with the name of whoever is to reply. Then all sit down, applaud, and wait for the toast-master or chairman to call on the person who is to respond. Sometimes this is done immediately, and for my part I prefer this, but sometimes, for a reason I cannot fathom, the chairman waits a few moments and then inquires solicitously if the responder is ready to reply.

By this method the excitement of the audience, stirred up by the proposer, has died down, the applause has ceased; everything is as flat as a pancake and the unlucky responder has to interest the audience all over again. But the chairman is in control and it is your duty to comply with his wishes.

An even worse delay is sometimes caused by the announcement of a break in the proceedings, so that those present may find their way to the cloakroom. This conduces to physical comfort, but not to mental comfort or enjoyment. It is all very well for the chairman to say briskly " an interval of ten minutes only "; once you have let your diners go you can't do anything to get them back again, and half an hour may easily be consumed before they return. Then they have to be settled down all over again. Meanwhile the speakers have lost all their enthusiasm for their speeches, and are to be found sitting gloomily around in the foyer in attitudes of despair. But if these Little Tiddleytown dinners have always had an interval, they will have an interval that night; take it pleasantly, and don't say a word about it until you have had a great success with your speech, when as the chairman congratulates you, you may murmur: " I'm so glad—I was just a little bit afraid—after an interval it's difficult to get the audience going, you know—but if you think it was all right. . . ." The chairman will gaze at you, startled, and reaffirm the tradition of the Little Tiddleytown dinners' interval; but you may have sown a seed of change.

Prize-Givings

Nothing is too good for children, and we all want to offer our young people the very best we can in the way of instruction and entertainment. But school prize-givings are in my experience very difficult occasions for the guest speaker.

The audience is exceedingly heterogeneous. The pupils range from twelve to seventeen in age, and this is just the period of their lives when they are " growing up " and changing most. A thought which is new and wonderful to the twelve-year-olds is a stale bore to the sixth form, and a thought which may have some point for the sixth-formers is beyond the reach of the younger children. Then, half the audience are parents, who view life from another very different point of view. How are you to find something to say which will interest all of them?

Platitudinous generalisations are despised by old and young alike, yet a talk on a specific " subject " is out of place because irrelevant; what you say must have some bearing on the situation in which all the children find themselves. Clearly something should be said about the proper attitude to life, or the uses of education. But these subjects have been spoken of, hundreds of times already. Therefore, only your truly personal views, carefully thought out, will have any value. What is the purpose of education? What is the use of books? What is the proper relation of industry to life? What is the proper balance between pleasure and work? How should we use standards of judgment, acquired in school, in the outside world? What are the especial dangers of contemporary life? What are its especial privileges? What are the mutual duties of parents and children? All these questions offer suitable subjects, but to think of something new and worthwhile to say on them requires, as I have said, a great deal of hard thought. Twenty minutes is about the right length—almost too ample in many cases—for a prize-giving. Interesting illustrations of what you are saying—anecdotes, humorous but not satiric—are indispensable; and you must get an anecdote into your address, very early.

Prize-givings are rather an ordeal for the children,

too. They have looked forward to this day for some time, and have been carefully drilled in the proper procedure. The thought of walking up the steps and across the platform, shaking hands and taking a prize in the other hand, may alarm them or may rejoice them, but it certainly excites. Very much washed and brushed and neatly garbed, they await the actual giving of the prizes in a state of tension.

At prize-givings, the main speech is always made after the Head's report. This is naturally long, and of great interest to the parents; the children listen to it attentively, from respect, but do not take it in very thoroughly, catching names they know here and there. But before the main speaker performs, the children have already sat still through the speech of the chairman of the Education Committee (or Board of Governors) and the Head's speech, and the younger ones may be getting a little restless. The guest speaker is now called on. At some prize-givings the speaker speaks first and then hands out the prizes; at others this procedure is reversed. I do not know which is worse for the speaker. If you speak first, the children are so keyed up by the thought of the prizes to come that they can hardly listen; if you speak after the prizes have been given, the children's day is over, they are relaxed, tired out, and give you but a dreamy and preoccupied ear, for they are longing to get home and show their prizes to their family. When you add to this the facts that the platform is crammed with local notabilities, the crowded hall is hot, the speaker has sat in public view for about three-quarters of an hour, constantly reminding himself (or more particularly herself) to sit up straight and keep the ankles neat, you will see that the speaker comes to a very difficult task with a tired mind. An early anecdote, to gain the pupils' interest and restore the speaker's confidence by their laughter, is indispensable. It must be a relevant anecdote, and if it can allude to young people in some way, that will catch your audience's attention. But let it be a true anecdote, something which really happened; a made-up anecdote always has a wrong note, a not-current-slang phraseology, and schoolchildren have very, very keen ears for falsities of this kind.

The most perfect anecdote for the purpose I ever heard was uttered in a prize-giving speech by a speaker whose name and status, I regret to say, I do not remember. Her purpose, as we presently discovered, was to urge her audience not to judge hastily, not to jump to conclusions before weighing all the evidence. This was the story. A boy went out to tea with a school-friend, and arrived home in a Rolls-Royce car driven by a chauffeur. His father thought it right to give him a warning. " Look, Tom," he said. " Your friend Jack is a nice lad, and I've no objection to your going about with him. But he obviously has a rich family. We are not rich; we can't run to Rolls-Royces. So don't get any wrong ideas." " Oh," said Tom, " Jack's father has two Rolls-Royces." His father blenched, and was just about to add: " Well, that makes it even worse! " when Tom added: " And a hearse."

You may guess how this story gripped the audience, how they woke up to listen to it, and roared with laughter at its conclusion. The rest of the speech was not up to this level of entertainment, but we listened attentively in the hope of something equally good.

Another difficulty about prize-giving speeches is that there is no recognised form of words with which to begin them. After you have reeled off the designations of the people you are addressing—there are always a great many local notabilities at a prize-giving, and they naturally like to be mentioned: " Mr. Chairman, Mr. Mayor, Madam Mayoress, Lord So-and-So, Headmaster, Tiddleytown Grammar School "—there is really nothing to do but go straight into your speech, unless there is some valid reason why you should be pleased to have been invited to make it. If you are an old pupil, or one of the Board of Governors, or have a boy or girl at the school, or longed to go to it when you were young, or went to school with the Head-mistress, then of course you may say so. Or if you are especially interested in education, or in the kind of educa-tion given at that particular school, of course say so. But don't begin: " It is a pleasure to me to be here this after-noon " unless it really *is* a pleasure—and if it is really a pleasure there will be a reason for it—for children are very quick to sense such hypocrisy. If there is no reason why you should feel pleasure, go straight ahead, and say: " I want (thought I would like) to talk to you this afternoon about. . . ."

And how are you to end a prize-giving speech? To sum up what you have been saying is not enough; it does not seem to acknowledge sufficiently the special character of the occasion. To congratulate the school on its achieve-ments during the last year is good, if you are speaking after the giving of the prizes; to wish the school well in its work and its play is a kindly thought; best of all is to ask that the school may have a day's holiday. Be sure to check this with the Head beforehand, of course.

One more very important word of advice. Do not call the pupils " children." The older pupils greatly dislike this. They are tired, too, of being referred to as " teen-agers," and not very fond of being called " pupils." Call them " the school," " the older members of the school," " the younger members of the school "; in this way you will not insult them.

Bazaars

Bazaar-openers are notorious for their feeble speeches, and indeed it is not easy to find anything interesting to say

115

on these occasions. But you would not be there unless you approved of the organisation for which the bazaar is to raise funds, so state your emphatic approval of this organisation, with a few statistics and anecdotes about the work the organisation does and why it needs to raise funds.

If the decorations of the hall are particularly original and attractive, mention them. It may be useful to mention the names of the various stalls—" There is a stall for haberdashery, one for home produce, a stall entirely devoted to handkerchiefs and buttons, and of course a white elephant stall." Be careful not to miss any stall from this list!

Any entertainments, catering arrangements and so on may similarly be mentioned, in a general way. If a target has been set for the bazaar, mention this target, and utter an emphatic wish for good luck in achieving it.

The proper conclusion to such speeches is to say: " I now declare this Bazaar open."

Five minutes is a suitable length for this kind of speech, though at a very large and formal bazaar ten minutes or even fifteen may be allowable. The greater the celebrity of the speaker, the longer the audience are willing to listen to him.

Weddings

Speeches at weddings are also often rather poor, but no-body minds this so long as they are sincere. The customary order of toasts is as follows:

Friend of family of bridegroom proposes health of bride and bridegroom.

Bridegroom replies.

Friend of family of bride proposes health of brides-maids.

Best man replies.

116

Friend of family of bridegroom proposes health of bride's father and mother, the host and hostess on the present occasion.

Bride's father replies.

Six speeches will occupy a good deal of time, so don't take too long over any of them. Since this is a very happy, long-to-be-remembered day in the lives of the wedded pair, let everything you say be as full of good will and affection as you can make it. Usually the friend who proposes the health of the bride and bridegroom is a real old family friend, a godfather perhaps or business partner who has known the bridegroom since he was a boy. But naturally the choice in this case depends on family circumstances. He says in effect what a fine young man the bridegroom is, touches on any special achievement of the bridegroom and anything of special interest in his future—his new appointment in Canada, or partnership in the family business, or promotion to foreman—and offers a most cordial welcome to the bride. A joke or so is not amiss, but please don't try to be too funny.

The bridegroom, responding, thanks the proposer of the toast, says what a lucky fellow he is to have won Mary— an anecdote here is pleasing—thanks all the guests and the givers of the splendid presents, and says a word of affection and gratitude to his own father and mother and the parents of his bride.

The main points to make about wedding speeches are:

Don't be too long.

Don't try to be too funny.

Remember it is not your day, but the bride and bridegroom's.

Don't say a word to cause distress.

Be sincere.

CHAPTER 10

Debating Societies

In the nineteenth century debating societies were a familiar feature of English life, and earnest young men developed in them their powers of thinking clearly and quickly, and speaking with effect. In the 1840's the Chartist movement laid its foundations and spread its doctrines from the London Debating Society. In the 1880's H. G. Wells, as he tells us in *Experiment in Autobiography*, learned to speak in the Imperial Institute debating society (from which he was once carried out struggling, by indignant members) and later crossed swords in debate with G. B. Shaw, the Webbs, and others at meetings of the Fabian society. To-day debating societies are chiefly found in universities—the Oxford Union is the prime example—and the upper forms of schools; national newspapers organise annual competitions to encourage university debating societies and this stimulation is valuable, while local competitions are often arranged between school teams of both sexes.

Procedure

The mode of procedure in a debating society is modelled on that of the House of Commons. A chairman presides (in the manner of the Speaker) impartially. He calls on the proposer to speak to the motion. Let us say that the motion selected by agreement beforehand is: " That this society/house/meeting approves of unilateral nuclear disarmament."

The proposer rises, states the motion, advances all the arguments in its favour, and concludes in some such sentences as: " It seems to me therefore that morality and

118

expediency are for once on the same side, and I call on those present to show their approval of this motion in an overwhelming majority."

The chairman then calls upon the opposer to oppose the motion. He does so, offering all his arguments, as that evil if it arises should be opposed, it cannot be opposed except by strength, and so on, and concludes by calling for a majority against the motion.

It is usual for a member in favour of the motion to speak next, to second the motion, and to be followed by a member against the motion. Then the meeting is thrown open to general discussion, and anyone may speak who catches the chairman's eye.

Variations of this procedure are of course often employed, and anyone invited to speak at such a society's meeting should inquire carefully which mode is employed, lest he inadvertently behave " out of order." Similarly a main speaker should inquire carefully about the length of speech required, as this is entirely a local affair, depending on local conditions.

Preparation

The two main speeches, by the proposer and opposer of the motion, are clearly more or less " set speeches "; they should be full of meat and carefully prepared. But the seconder and second opposer are much more free, and though they should have thought out what they believe on the matter and prepared one or two cogent arguments on their side, their effectiveness as speakers will depend largely on picking holes in the previous speeches of their opponents. " Hole-picking " is necessarily impromptu, and this opportunity for quick thought and impromptu speech is the most valuable part of a debating society, for here you are able to try out your abilities at impromptu speech, without risking any public disaster. Indeed, if a seconder's speech is too well prepared, too little impromptu, it will be disliked as tedious and irrelevant, while a dashing impromptu will be admired as courageous. A speaker in a debate following a speaker with whom he disagrees should always begin by a little hole-picking, even if he then retires to the safety of his prepared arguments.

Wells's account of the Imperial Institute (later the University of London) debating society meetings, which were held in an underground lecture room, is as follows:

" The usual formula was a paper, for half an hour or so, a reply and then promiscuous discussion. Those who lacked the courage to speak, interjected observations, made sudden outcries or hammered the desks. The desks indeed were hammered until the ink jumped out of the pots."

This shows exactly the ladder of progress in such a society. The newly joined member at first hammers the desk, then finds himself shouting: " No! " Once he has heard his own voice giving public utterance in a public assembly, his fear of this phenomenon is gone, and he is soon crying: " But that is a fallacy, Mr. Chairman! " From this whole sentence he gains courage to leap up and address the chairman formally: " Mr. Chairman, the figures given in the last published analysis do not support the speaker's view. . . ."

For any young man or woman who wishes to undertake a political career, membership of a debating society is— I will not say indispensable—but extremely helpful.

For politics are essentially a debate about the best way of arranging the life of the community. You believe in one mode of arrangement, and wish to persuade your hearers to believe in it too; your opponent believes in another mode of arrangement; it is considered to be your duty to point out all the fallacies, the weaknesses, in his chosen mode, to trip him up, to catch him out. Personally I dislike this way of proceeding; I have no objection to correcting errors or to propagating my own views, but to try deliberately to humiliate another human being is foreign to my nature, and I dislike seeing it attempted, whether on the platform or the television screen. I prefer discussion to debate. But there are times when even the mildest of us has to fight, to attack abuses, to defend the innocent; to have learned the habit of quick repartee, of telling phrase, of crushing retort, is valuable, provided its employment is restricted to occasions when you have a definite opponent, and his arguments deserve defeat.

EPILOGUE

H. G. Wells's account of himself speaking at a Fabian meeting may perhaps amuse you:

" Myself speaking haltingly on the verge of the inaudible, addressing my tie through a cascade moustache that was of no sort of help at all, correcting myself as though I were a manuscript under treatment, making ill-judged departures into parenthesis . . ."

It is precisely to eliminate these distracting habits that this book has been written.

Index

123